"This book gives testimony t[...] over many years to his exter[...] Each vignette provides insig[...] daily on the streets of our cities. It also offers us a portrait of Christian dedication in the selfless service of one man to his community. This is a recommended read for anyone interested in one of the most pressing issues of our time."

—**Dennis M. Anholt**, retired professor, University of Victoria

"Rev. Al has a way of seeing the essence of the divine in every human. This book is a testimony to his deeply spiritual connection to humanity in all our varied and not always pretty manifestations."

—**Harry Brechner**, rabbi, Congregation Emanu-El

"*Muddy Water* is a must-read. The stories have substance; they challenge the church and all of us to better understand the men and women living on the streets, since their stories are intertwined with ours. As a First Nations leader, I thank Rev. Allen Tysick for bringing these stories to life."

—**George Jr. Hunt**, Kwa-guilth artist and elder

"Informed by the author's Christian faith, suffused with ecumenical compassion, and leavened with humor, this book is a testament to resilience, strength, wisdom and humanity in the face of suffering. An entertaining read, it is also a document of redemption."

—**Gabor Maté**, author of *The Myth of Normal: Trauma, Illness and Healing in a Toxic Culture*

"*Muddy Water* takes us to the streets with Rev. Al as he walks beside those who live on the margins of our society. I loved this collection of modern-day parables. It is street scripture that will touch your heart and open your mind, as it pricks your conscience. This should be required reading for all politicians. It's storytelling at its best!"

—**Jo-Ann Roberts**, author of *Storm the Ballot Box: Starting a Voting Revolution before It's Too Late*

"You will want to reach in and embrace Rev. Al's street family as your own. You can't read this raw and honest portrayal of street ministry without being touched by the beauty and wisdom of individuals most of us ignore. At once funny, heartbreaking, and infuriating, you will run the gamut of human emotions as you turn each page. This book is a haunting eye-opener and should be required reading for everyone."

—**SILVIA FIORITA SMITH**, author of *Figs beneath the Snow: Unearthing the Poetry*

"Rev. Al offers a unique window into the lives of people living on the street. For him, the homeless are people to love and embrace—not a problem to be solved. Prepare to be touched and transformed."

—**LEE HANES**, retired social worker

"Rev. Al, as he is fondly called, is a powerful storyteller! In this lifetime of street ministry, he has penetrated through muddy waters as though 'through a glass darkly' and peers into the heart and soul of the human person. Al reaches into the depths of human suffering endured by persons living on the street, inviting and challenging us to embrace their suffering as our own. Al leads us to see with the heart, to see with God's eyes, and to humbly sit at the table and listen to wisdom from the street. At Rev. Al's table, there is no us and them—there is only shared pain, joy, agony and hope."

—**JOYCE HARRIS**, SSA, canonical co-leader, Roman Catholic Sisters of St. Ann

"*Muddy Water* is a true testament to the love and compassion of its writer, Rev. Al Tysick. He earned the trust and respect of so many in our community and beyond, for the person he is and for the work he has done. During my twenty years as a Victoria city councilor, I learned from him. Every person has their own story if we only take the time to listen. *Muddy Water* is essential reading for anyone who wants to better understand the issue of homelessness."

—**CHARLAYNE THORNTON-JOE**, retired Victoria city councilor

Muddy Water

Muddy Water

Stories from the Street

AL TYSICK

Illustrations by Elfrida Schragen

RESOURCE *Publications* · Eugene, Oregon

MUDDY WATER
Stories from the Street

Copyright © 2024 Al Tysick. All rights reserved. Except for brief quotations in critical publications or reviews, no part of this book may be reproduced in any manner without prior written permission from the publisher. Write: Permissions, Wipf and Stock Publishers, 199 W. 8th Ave., Suite 3, Eugene, OR 97401.

Resource Publications
An Imprint of Wipf and Stock Publishers
199 W. 8th Ave., Suite 3
Eugene, OR 97401

www.wipfandstock.com

PAPERBACK ISBN: 979-8-3852-1501-0
HARDCOVER ISBN: 979-8-3852-1502-7
EBOOK ISBN: 979-8-3852-1503-4

VERSION NUMBER 05/24/24

Scripture quotations marked (NKJV) are taken from the Holy Bible, New King James Version®. Copyright © 1982 by Thomas Nelson. Used by permission. All rights reserved.

Scripture quotations marked ASV are taken from American Standard Version, 1901 (in public domain).

Dedicated to my soulmate,
friend, and loving wife,
Mary Hanes Tysick,
who provided
innumerable types of support
as I prepared this book

Contents

Illustrations | xi
Preface: Who Is Al Tysick? | xiii
Acknowledgments | xvii
Introduction: Canada Day | xxi

Section I: Muddy Water

1   Muddy Water | 3
2   Vivacious | 6
3   Life Takes Many Turns | 8
4   Who Can I Blame? | 10
5   The Dragon Collector | 14
6   Cry of Lament | 19
7   The Victorias | 21
8   Emmanuel | 24
9   Missing | 27
10 Tell Him to Put His Shirt On | 28
11 I'm Lonely | 31
12 Just His Face | 34
13 Wandering Spirit | 36
14 The Wilted Flower | 40
15 Panhandling | 42
16 A Sculpture | 46
17 Compassion and Humanity | 49
18 Cold Wind | 52
19 Island Paradise | 54

Section II: Transformation: Dealing with Death

20 Suicide | 59
21 Oh Death, Where's Your Sting? | 61
22 Sombrio Beach | 65
23 Free at Last | 68
24 Fentanyl | 71
25 Give Me Grace | 73
26 Kaleidoscopic Eyes | 76
27 Jim | 79
28 A Cry in the Night | 82
29 The Lone Wolf | 84
30 Red Feather | 86
31 It's All a Plan | 89
32 James | 92
33 Obstacles | 94
34 The Dragon's Power | 97
35 The Flame That Consumes | 99

Section III: Church / Street Ministry

36 The Gift of a Diamond | 105
37 Easter Story | 108
38 Hear My Prayer | 110
39 The Push | 112
40 Exorcism | 115
41 Judgment | 120
42 The Tea Room | 124
43 Harley's Untimely Death | 129
44 Mother Mary Chamunda | 131
45 Burning Eyes | 133
46 The Prayer | 137
47 Shopping Cart | 140
48 My Argument | 143

Section IV: Articles and Speeches

49 Do You Have Your Heart On? | 147
50 Betty | 149
51 The Unknown Strangers | 151

52	The Gift of Christmas	153
53	A Place of Belonging	155
54	Hopes and Dreams	157
55	A Spiritual Question	159
56	The Pitcher	162
57	A Tribute to Melba Markel	164
58	An Angel of a Different Sort	167
59	Not Alone	170
60	Cinderella and the Shoe	173
61	Standing in the Rain	175
62	Theology	178

Section V: Holy Rage

63	Sky's Story	183
64	The Old Man	185
65	Sitting on the Fence	188
66	Alley of Death	191
67	An Emergency	194
68	Move On	196
69	Are You Useless Too?	199
70	I Walk Alone	201
71	Oliver	203
72	We Can No Longer Be Silent	206

Bibliography | 209

Illustrations

ILLUSTRATIONS ARE BY VICTORIA artist Elfrida Schragen, who previously completed three successful fund raisers for Our Place. Her portraits of homeless people hang in many homes and businesses, plus a gallery at Our Place. These book sketches add a new dimension to the words of Rev. Al Tysick.

Elfrida is a parent, teacher, social worker, farmer, and cellist, as well as an artist.

Web site: www.elfridasart.com

Preface
Who Is Al Tysick?

WITHIN THIS BOOK, IN the silence between the words, is a new way to redefine and recreate the *church*, provided by voices from the prophets outside the walls of the institution. The voice of the Creator can be heard by those who have ears to listen. One does not need to be *religious* in order to hear and act upon these thoughts.

Preface

I was born in July 1946. My mother was a devout Catholic who did not feel worthy to pray directly to God, so she prayed to Mother Mary. We lived on welfare—the crumbs that fell from the rich person's table. My mother didn't notice our stark poverty against the church's extreme wealth. Her conservative, fundamental faith I believed fully until I was 11 years old.

I had just turned 11, and it was three days before *Welfare Day*. I opened all our cupboard doors; they were empty. I got on my knees and asked my mother's God to put food on our table—just enough for my three younger sisters. The next morning, the cupboards were still empty. I tearfully went to the store and stole a large jar of peanut butter, a loaf of bread, a quart of milk, a can of beans, and some bologna. That day my mother's God died within me, and I became open to other avenues of belief.

My father was a violent alcoholic who beat me often as a child, and I came to hate him. Growing up on the street, I would rather fight than eat. One day I got into a fight with a bigger older boy, and when he was on the ground bleeding, someone pulled me off him. I saw him dazed and bloodied, and I realized that I could have killed him. I was becoming my father! I cried as I asked him to forgive me. That day, I put down my fist and began to use my brain.

Education was a struggle since I suffer from dyslexia. Despite that, I graduated from Carlton University with a BSc., initially working at the National Research Council in the mechanical engineering department for five years. Feeling a call to be ordained in the church, at night school I received a BA in religious studies. I then went to McGill University for a B.Th., later being ordained by the United Church of Canada. I left my paid ministry with the fine people of Hulbert Valley and Brinston United Churches, south of Ottawa near the St. Lawrence River, after ten years of service there. There was a pocket of rural poverty located in nearby Dundela, such as I had never seen before, and it inspired a dramatic change.

On July 1, 1989, The House of Lazarus was created in a Dundela church that had been abandoned for at least 20 years. The building structure was sound, but it had no water, heat, electricity, nor a washroom, and I had no salary. Three women were the foundation of the House of Lazarus: Melba Markell, Myra Fawcett, and Beth McGrath. I was fed at the tables of the poor; I was taken care of by the poor. I went to minister to them, and they ministered to my St. Bernard dog Cesar and to me. I came to educate; then they educated me. Among other activities, I helped the community build 32 homes.

Preface

After five years there, I was called by the United Church of Canada to be the Executive Director of The Open Door, a ministry of the Victoria Presbytery among the homeless, due to the retirement of Lawrence Moon. At the Open Door and its successor, Our Place, I continued living out my calling, including subsequent work with the Victoria Dandelion Society. The stories you'll find in this book largely come from that profound time in the city of Victoria, British Columbia, Canada.

The Open Door was a drop-in center whose mission statement read: "The Open Door offers unconditional love in a nonjudgmental way for all." When I read that statement, I knew that it was God calling me in full joy to give my life to this ministry. Like the House of Lazarus, I came to minister to the poor, and the poor ministered to me. I came to give my life to them, and they gave their lives to me.

Nearby was the Upper Room, a ministry of the combined Presbyterian and Anglican churches that fed and housed the homeless every day. The Executive Director was Rev. David Stewart. He and I came to have a sincere respect for one another as we became close friends and shared laughter, tears, and deep faith. That friendship and the courage of both boards merged into Our Place: a multi-purpose service to the homeless. I became the Executive Director when David reached 65.

At my own 65 years young, another call came from a modern-day prophet named Vince, an Inuit who lived in a doorway on Fort Street for most of his adult life. That day he was sitting cross-legged, and I sat beside him. An older lady passed by, and I put out my empty hand. She put 50 cents into it and walked on. I smiled and gave the coins to Vince, who held the money in the palm of his hand, staring at it for the longest time. Finally, he looked into my eyes.

"Rev, it's time you leave Our Place and come to the street to begin your holy calling."

Without another word, he got to his feet and walked away.

That day I put together my 3-month notice of resignation and drove it to the home of Dr. Dennis Anholt, Chair of the Our Place Board. I then went to see my good friend Ned Easton and asked him if he'd help me form a new street-oriented organization called the Dandelion Society.

Without question, he responded, "It's about time—I start today."

Ned and I called capable people to form the first board of the Victoria Dandelion Society: Anna Stella Jazlowiecki, Ned Easton (Chair), E. Al Crippen, Paul Jenkins, Pat Vickers, Marcus Oppenheimer, Mike Nelson,

Arthur Wright. I also have special memories of the late Ann Cameron, who passed away during her time as Chair of the board.

So began another ministry in faith, initially without a salary.

Along the way, I married my wonderful wife, Mary Hanes. Actually, I married her twice: once as a minister, and once after she became a widow! We have three grown children and some delightful grandchildren, too. I'm grateful for the balance and inspiration that they constantly provide.

This book is about faith and a new vision of the church. It comes from the prophetic voices of the poor outside the church walls, who are angels of a different sort. Thanks go out to my street family for having the courage to push me into the muddy water of faith!

The following *Addendum* is from some of Al's friends, who want readers to know a few other things:

Education also includes:

Certifications: Marriage Counseling, Drug and Alcohol, Anger Management, Suicide Prevention.

Honorary BA, School of Social Work, University of Victoria.

Other activities:

Leadership (often as Founder): Lateral Thinkers; Legal Aid Services in Cornwall, Ontario; Seaway Valley Presbytery; Council of Greater Victoria Coalition to End Homelessness; Victoria Downtown Service Providers; Co-convenor of United Church of Canada national *Energy from the Edges* conference, with Fay Wakeling and Barry Morris.

Other honors:

Citizen of the Year, Matilde Township, Ontario; Citizen of the Year, Victoria, British Columbia; Mayor's Medal Award, City of Victoria, British Columbia; Queen's Jubilee Medal; Recognized by the Songhees First Nation; Friend of the Ahousaht First Nation; Queen Elizabeth II's Platinum Jubilee Medallion (2022)

Acknowledgments

I ACKNOWLEDGE AND HONOR the Coast Salish people, especially Xwsepsum (Esquimalt), Lekwungen (Songhees), Sc'ianew (Beecher Bay) and T'Souke (Sooke), for their gracious hospitality on the unceded territory where the book Muddy Water came to birth.

Special thanks go to the Ahousaht Nation, particularly Simon Louie and family. They taught me so much about my ignorance as a privileged white man and introduced me to their rich culture. I'm grateful also to Kwa-guilth artist George Jr. Hunt, who not only introduced me to his master carving but also shared the heartbeat of his culture.

Thank you to my family and dear associates for support and encouragement:

Mary Hanes Tysick

Lee Hanes

Jordan and Katherin Cooper

Jared Cooper and Jacklyn Evans

Alicia Tysick and Noah Yatsko

Grandchildren Everett and Charlie Cooper

Sisters Sylvia Van der Stegen, Barbara Ann Weeks, Florence Sayeau, and Wendy Osborne

Extended family Molly Cameron & Dan Cameron

Greg Attewell

Acknowledgments

The book team:

This book would not have been possible without the team of people I gathered around me. It is genuinely *our* book. These team members have donated their time and talent, wishing for all book proceeds to go to charity.

Elfrida Schragen, Illustrator

Connie Foss More, Book Coordinator and Managing Editor

Rick Mickelson, Assistant Editor

Bruce More, Computer craftsman, including pre-publication layout

Paul Jenkins, Marketing Coordinator

Gene Miller, Publicist

History is a big part of this book. Looking back, thanks go to:

The United Church of Canada, especially the Victoria Presbytery, the Victoria Open Door ministry boards, and particularly Ann Beal and Audrey McClennan for inviting me to be the Executive Director.

Our Place: Dr. Robert (Robin) Krause, a friend and Chair of the Open Door ministry, who negotiated the amalgamation of the Open Door and the Upper Room to become Our Place Society in 2005. John Ronald, Chair of the Upper Room and the first Our Place Chair. He also negotiated the amalgamation; the new Our Place building opened on Pandora Avenue in 2007. Alan Lowe, former Victoria Mayor, whose courage and leadership brought federal and provincial governments to financially support the building of Our Place Society. The late Reverend David Stewart, a personal friend and my partner as we dreamed dreams together—without David, Our Place would not have been possible. The current leadership and staff caringly continue the work and vision of these predecessors.

Dandelion Society: Mary North and Margaret North, who were instrumental in bringing the society to birth. The board members, especially past Chairs Ned Easton, Brennen Chow, and the late Ann Cameron.

The many *donors* of all ages who supported the Open Door ministry, Our Place Society, and the Dandelion Society during my 30 years of leadership. I thank you all! There are specific generous families that supported Our Place and the Dandelion Society throughout my leadership and wish to remain anonymous: please accept my enduring gratitude.

Acknowledgments

The staff of Royal Jubilee and Victoria General hospitals, for saving the lives of so many of my street family over the years.

The Victoria Police Department members for the compassion, kindness, and generosity they have shown.

The Vancouver Island Regional Library Sooke Branch, for its support and welcome, as a table there seemingly became my office while the book was created.

People who wrote pre-publication endorsements of the book, helping it to be accepted by a publisher and subsequently marketed to readers:

- Dennis M. Anholt, Ph.D.: Retired Professor, University of Victoria. Past Chair of the Our Place Society, past Chair of Threshold Housing Society
- Rabbi Harry Brechner: Congregation Emanu-El, Victoria, British Columbia
- Lee Hanes: Retired Social Worker, Rehabilitation Counsellor, and Probation Officer
- Joyce Harris, SSA: Canonical Co-Leader, Roman Catholic Sisters of St. Ann
- George Jr. Hunt: Kwa-guilth artist and elder
- Gabor Maté M.D.: Author, *The Myth of Normal: Trauma, Illness and Healing in a Toxic Culture*
- Jo-Ann Roberts: Leader, Writer, Broadcaster; MFA in Creative Non-fiction
- Silvia Fiorita Smith: Author of *Figs Beneath the Snow: Unearthing the Poetry*
- Charlayne Thornton-Joe: Victoria City Councillor (retired)

I am grateful that Wipf and Stock Publishers believe in this book and want others to experience it.

Connie More deserves my most profound appreciation as my friend and managing editor; we laughed and cried together as the book came to life.

Thanks to you, the reader. May this book enrich and challenge your understanding of those living in poverty and without homes.

To all the men and women who struggle with addictions, mental health, loneliness, and/or homelessness who told me their stories and let me into their lives, my deepest thanks. All I have is because of you.

Introduction
Canada Day

CANADA DAY IS NORMALLY a day of celebration for the wonderful things this country has achieved. However, the recent discoveries of hundreds of children's graves on the grounds of our old residential schools have shaken us to the core.

We must commit to never forgetting our history, and never letting anything like this happen again. We must free ourselves and our god of power, injustice, inequality, and poverty. We must take the road less travelled: to where poverty has ended and the environment leads us. We need a country where all votes matter in a proportional representation system, and where everyone has a guaranteed livable income. In our multicultural country, we all need respect and a voice.

I remain optimistic because First Nations people have taught me the importance of storytelling. Their stories give me hope and show that greed will destroy us all if we place profits above our shared humanity. As we discover more graves of Indigenous children, we must ask ourselves, "Why is the system not changing for everyone"?

As I sit in my cozy chair in my comfortable home, I wonder why it is not time for others to change the world. Then the hard question comes back: what am I doing to change the world?

> Jesus asked Simon Peter 3 times: "Do you love me?
> Each time, Simon Peter replied, "Yes, Lord, you know that I love you!"
> Jesus replied, "Feed my sheep."
> Paraphrased from John 21:15–17 (NKJV)

Introduction

So now I ask, what more can I do; how can I help? Perhaps the pen *is* mightier than the sword. Yes, I'm retired and in my seventies; I can no longer carry the heavy load. I've given my life to the poor, the addicted, the mentally ill, and the lonely. Maybe now, from my armchair, I can still work to bring about change by humbly telling their stories. Inspired by the tales the First Nations have taught me, often told and retold, I offer my sincere views of the street.

I was invited to a Reconciliation gathering one day from 7 am to 9 pm, put on by the Ahousaht Nation. A White man asked me, "When will we earn their forgiveness so that we can move on"?

Forgiveness is not easy; for many, it may be impossible. When we read about forgiveness, we are told it frees and liberates us. It lets go of resentment, bitterness, and anger, sometimes even hatred. However, it can also bring our history back to the conscious mind and open up old wounds. Forgiveness is a process that, for many, is too painful a road to travel. For others, it is too easy to say and often has no substance.

That is why I like the word Reconciliation. Within the meaning are time, story, liaising, learning, pain, and the rebuilding of First Nations culture.

Reconciliation is a long journey in the forced dark where individuals, First Nations, White *settlers*, and others travel back to our oppressive history of colonization to face the pain and its lasting effect on Indigenous people. Reconciliation tells the stories of the ancestors and their survivors. Their historical journeys relive their pain and the discrimination they faced and still face today. The stories, the dances, the drums, and the art tell of the many individuals, families, and innocent children whose lives have been taken.

At another Reconciliation gathering, a White man publicly asked, "I keep hearing the same story. Will we ever move on"?

There was an awkward silence in the hall. Finally, an Indigenous woman elder stood up by her wheelchair and spoke. "I have listened to your biblical story throughout my life." She paused, regained control of her emotions, and continued, "Why should our story be any different"?

Unlike forgiveness, reconciliation has no precise end. It is rather about healing, and that is only possible if we all dare to take this long journey together. Will you come with us? Everyone is welcome.

SECTION I

Muddy Water

1

Muddy Water

A COLD WIND FROM the north was persistent as I walked along the Inner Harbor one January morning. I'd received a call from the police asking me if I'd check on the residents of a tent down there. Rain had been continually falling for three days, and the harbor was abandoned. Many luxurious yachts were tied to the dock, covered with expensive hand-made tarps. A rare Viking longboat in all its splendor was also moored there that morning. Their residents, for the most part, were sleeping in one of the expensive hotels along the quay.

In Victoria, regardless of anyone's political stripe, there's a huge gap between the rich and the poor that is particularly visible on the Inner Harbor with the Empress Hotel in its background. Whereas most of the world's religions promote some version of *this* Golden Rule: "Do unto others as you would have them do unto you", this harbor scene reminded me of a different yet pervasive Golden Rule: "Those who have the gold make the rules".

I could see a small green tent in the distance. As I approached it, a light flickering inside was visible, so I announced my arrival.

"Hi, it's Rev Al. Can I bring you a coffee"?

A young man unzipped the tent and came out to greet me. He was shorter than most, with broad shoulders. He had large hands and a massive head of hair that sprang out in all directions, making him look like Einstein. Behind him came a taller man with an unusually long neck and bulging eyes. The third person in that tent was a young woman about twenty-five years old, with long flowing red hair matching her facial freckles, and big hazel eyes.

Section I: Muddy Water

I noticed that her eyes were particularly sad. She never smiled or spoke a word and looked sickly. Her skin was pale, and she was very thin. The shorter man spoke for them in a distinctly Italian accent.

"Father, we know about your work but never believed we'd be fortunate enough to meet you. We heard about you first in Montreal from a priest we met there, and then again in Vancouver from a homeless man."

The young woman stepped forward and hugged me—then the other two joined her. They all spoke broken English with Italian accents. I knew the *lingo* well because, as a boy, I lived near Preston Street in Ottawa, often called little Italy. It was a friendly neighborhood that was perfect for me as a boy. My best friend was Amamario, an Italian child. His family fed me often and taught me to laugh out loud. Late at night, we'd all sit on their veranda listening to his grandfather play the accordion. We'd sing old Italian songs that came from their motherland, and all the neighbors would join in. Judgment, finances, and cultural differences gave way to song.

"Can I help you in any way"? I asked.

The taller man answered, "Yes, Father, you can bless us on our journey." His bulging eyes made this request even more earnest.

The short man interrupted, "It's rude of us not to have shared our names! I'm Abramo, my brother is Basilio, and our sister's name is Maria. We're from Italy—but I guess you know that"! They all then burst into laughter. "Two months ago, we landed in Montreal because we wanted to see Canada. Today we're leaving for Tofino to have a look at Long Beach and all the big evergreen trees there. Your country is *giganteso*," said Ambramo.

"Everything's so big," responded his brother. "We've worked for a few days as casual laborers while we hitchhiked across the country."

"Why did you choose to come during our rainy season"? I asked.

"I have stage three cancer," replied Maria. "My doctor told me that I have only six months to live. When my brothers heard that diagnosis, they remembered that one of my childhood dreams was to see Canada. They both quit their jobs and bought three return tickets to this country so my wish could come true. We decided to travel during the first three months because I didn't know if I'd be strong enough to travel in the last three months."

After a long silence, I cried out to the suffering Christ, "Lord, have mercy."

I gave them each a cup of coffee, some new socks, sleeping bags, and several freshly baked cookies. They were very grateful. As I was about to leave, Maria knelt down on both her knees.

"Father," she said, "Please don't go without blessing us."

Then her brothers knelt beside her. With that, I knelt on the ground, putting both my knees in a puddle of muddy water, and I reached out to them. We held hands.

> God of love, walk with Maria, Basilio, and Abramo on their spiritual journey. Help them discover you in every leaf and rock in our nation. May they discover the spirit of our First Nations people as they travel over traditional lands. May every step they take on Mother Earth be healing and reveal your love, which is eternal. May the love that they've shown towards one another be shining examples to all our people. May they not only visit Canada but leave their spirit of love behind for us all to experience. Dear Lord, may Maria come to understand that this is not a gift that her brothers are giving her, but rather a gift she gave to them that will remain as a treasured memory throughout their entire lives. May this gift strengthen and bless them all.

Then I slipped my fingers into the muddy puddle of water beneath my knees, and I put the sign of the cross on each of their foreheads. It was holy water as if given by the hand of God.

As I was walking away from them, it came to mind that my ministry on the street has always been a little muddy: not at all orthodox, and outside the Christian church's policies, procedures, and doctrine.

2

Vivacious

THE STORIES OF THE street are like night itself—given life in the shadows of darkness, fed by poverty, addictions, poor mental health, and loneliness. But sometimes a flower blooms in the night.

Her mother raised her against all odds in Surrey, British Columbia. They lived on welfare and were as poor as can be. She was born in a rooming house, and there were no doctors or nurses in attendance. Rooming houses, motel rooms, and homeless shelters were where they laid their heads. She was vivacious, strong, bold, and very smart. She was homeschooled by her mother and graduated with top honors from Grade 12.

However, her mother died the following year. The funeral was held at a drop-in center for homeless people, where we all said our goodbyes. At the gravesite, the daughter was the last to leave. Tears engulfed her, raining down her face.

Her mother was all she had; they had been inseparable. Only in the darkness of death would separation be found. She walked the streets that dark night, talking to her mother as she used to do. Exhaustion overtook her, so she lay down on a bench in the early morning light.

Days later she found me and asked me to sit on a hill with her at the Inner Harbor. It's a day I'll never forget.

"Tell me the old stories of my mother that I don't know," she asked. "Tell me the truth, as hard as it may be."

There were many stories I could have shared, but I told her this one: "You were about sixteen years old on a stormy November evening. You slept beside her in the shelter that night, sharing a blanket on the floor. She was brushing her hair as you slept. She saw me walk by and did not miss a beat."

"She's brighter than most," your mother said out loud. "She's going to be richer than the rest."

Suddenly the young woman cried out to me loudly, "A lawyer! That's what I'll become."

She filled out an application and mailed it. Weeks later, she accepted a grant from the university. When I drove her to the Greyhound bus station, others joined me in waving goodbye as she headed to Ottawa.

Those were the days before computers, texts, emails, Twitter (X) or Zoom, so over the years, we lost contact with one another. But I'm certain that on a stage at the University of Ottawa one spring, a flower bloomed in spite of the darkness.

3

Life Takes Many Turns

Life takes many turns,
Decisions are made,
Directions are set,
Then suddenly, there's a turn in the road.

The years pass,
Aging stops for nothing.
We turn around,
And we are old.

We can clearly see our history,
And some of the turns we regret.

Some of the hills
That we never thought we could conquer
Now stand behind us.

Yet in life, every turn was a teaching.
Right or wrong, failure or success,
We learned something about ourselves.

The turns in the road are not bound by time.
Just when we thought the road was finally leading to the valley,
We stand up, and in front of us is yet another obstacle.

Life Takes Many Turns

Now we have our toolbox filled with the experiences of life.
Our failures have taught us perhaps more than our successes.

The young man still lives inside us,
Yet the mirror reflects the old man in front of us.

Can we climb that new hill?
All common sense would say "no";
All experience would say, "Walk the other way."
Yet we put one foot in front of the other to make it to the top of the hill.

It is not as important as it was when we were young.
All that matters now is our integrity.

4

Who Can I Blame?

Who can I blame?
When a man is drunk and lonely,
He needs to find the answer to a question that is haunting him.

It was January and snow covered the ground.
He stumbled into the shelter I was operating that night.
I handed him a coffee to warm his freezing hands.
Others had fallen asleep, and the snow was still coming down.
He sat down at a table, looking for me to acknowledge the hope still alive in his heart.

"Father," he said, as he acknowledged me with respect,
"I've sinned; please ask Mother Mary to forgive me."

Then he began:

Who can I blame?

Can I blame my mother, who was addicted at my birth?
Can I blame my father, who beat me as a child?
Can I blame my teacher, who told me I was stupid?

Who can I blame?

Who Can I Blame?

Can I blame my wife, who left me for another,
Leaving two children behind in her wake?
Can I blame my landlord,
Who evicted us on a cold November night?
Can I blame my dealer who sold me a hot cap?

Who can I blame?

When I was in the hospital with an infection in my lung,
The system came to take away my children.
They were only six and eight years old.
That night is forever ingrained in my mind, and
I will never forget it.
When I left the hospital, my apartment was empty—my children gone!

Section I: Muddy Water

Who can I blame?

A judge sentenced me to two years for dealing fentanyl,
So, I could not see my children.
The two years passed quickly.

My addiction was by then under control, I believed.
But on my release day, I had no place to go.
The parole officer gave me a piece of paper
Saying the Salvation Army was offering me a bed.
Lying angry and wounded in their dorm that night, tears ran down my face.
I was alone again.
No one cared a damn about me.
The fellow in the next bunk cracked open a new bottle
And offered me a drink.
With no thought or consideration, I put the bottle to my lips.

Who could I blame?

A year later the rain was pouring down, and
The answer to my question came to me out of a drunken rage.
An old Newfoundland guy had offered me his bottle.
We sat down to drink.
We were sitting in an alley on Hastings behind a dumpster.
It was the only shelter we could find.

I told him my story.
It was full of anger, hatred, and revenge.
He opened up another bottle and took another swig.
As he handed me the bottle, tears welled in his eyes.

"Your story is missing something:
The question that haunts you will never be answered until you face the truth.
Who's to blame, you ask?
You quickly blame others,
Pointing out their faults."

Who Can I Blame?

Tears ran into the deep furrows of his face.
Then he poked two large fingers into my chest and spoke.

"You blame others and there may be some truth there.
But as you point one finger at them, four fingers point back at you.
Our answers are not in the bottle we both have sucked on this night,
The answer is within us.
And that's the hardest place to look."

Then he grabbed the bottle and turned his back on me.
Leaving the alley, he yelled.
"Who's to blame?
You and I are to blame,
Don't you see"?

5

The Dragon Collector

To look at him would bring fear into the hearts of many. He was muscular and bigger than most men. On his large right bicep, he had a tattoo of the skull of a pig. On his left bicep, a tattoo of the face of Satan could be seen, over crossbones.

For many years I'd seen him only from a distance. He'd be in his new Mercedes at the side of the road with my street family gathered around buying his products: heroin, cocaine, crystal meth, and opium. I also occasionally heard about him from someone I was visiting in the hospital. They'd tell me that they owed him money, and how he'd always find them when they were alone and then beat them. He wished to leave a clear message for others who didn't pay for his products.

He was known on the street as the Dragon Collector, a name he'd apparently given himself after he got the fire-breathing dragon tattoo. That tattoo ran the entire length of his body, starting at his neck, then down his back with a tail wrapping itself around the bottom of his right leg. Anyone who didn't pay for his drugs soon encountered a breath of fire upon them.

I visited many folks in the hospital bearing the wounds and skewers of his fire: broken arms, jaws, noses, legs, ribs, and even insides. His fire was felt and feared by many, and his punishment was quick and brutal. I particularly remember one man who I visited in intensive care for days. It was uncertain whether he'd live or die, and when he did come out of the coma, he had permanent brain damage.

But he said to me, "The Dragon Collector told me to pay up for several days, but I kept acting tough, like a big shot. I pushed him down, spit on him, and told him to get lost. When he got up off the ground, he told me, 'You've got one month to pay up; then all will be forgotten.'"

"Exactly one month later, I was walking home late one night. I noticed that his car was parked in front of my apartment. I saw him get out of it, but that's all I can remember. There were no witnesses."

Life on the street is not glamorous, pretty, or romantic. A fight on the street is nothing like the ones on TV. When someone is hit by a baseball bat, he goes down. When he's hit on the jaw, nose, or throat, he doesn't get back up. As a minister, I witness these kinds of violent acts all the time. I see the pain, suffering, and death of many who I've come to love. Drug and alcohol addiction is a one-way street to hell on earth.

One chilly early morning, as rain persistently pounded the ground, I pulled up to one of my usual stops, to visit the homeless people who sleep there during the night. About thirty men and women were waiting for me. Three of them were passed out on the sidewalk with no blankets to cover them, and they lay there soaking wet. Two of the others were arguing, and I saw another man bent over in extreme pain. Then I noticed the Dragon Collector standing off to the side, staring in my direction. He was wearing very expensive jewelry: two impressive gold chains hanging around his neck and several large gold rings set with precious stones on his fingers.

Just then, one of the men vomited all over me and himself. I could see the Dragon Collector watching me as I carefully lifted the sick man into my van so that I could get him warm.

In spite of my calling to follow Christ, in spite of my conviction to forgive, in spite of my years in the street ministry, I still struggle at times to forgive and forget the trespasses of some of my street family. On that day, I could feel my resentment and judgment towards the Dragon Collector that had built up over years. Then the question that Jesus asked Simon Peter three times came into my conscious mind, from John 21:15–17 NKJV:

"Do you love me?"

All of a sudden, I looked up and saw the Dragon Collector standing right in front of me. Abruptly he said, "I need to see you before you leave."

My heart began to pound. My feelings were a mixture of fear and compassion. As we walked away from the crowd, he followed me, so I asked him how I could help him.

Section I: Muddy Water

"I've been in jail for the last four months. During that time, I was informed that my dad, who had been living in Halifax, had committed suicide. He hanged himself in a back alley just a block away from the house he was born in. Not one person attended his funeral. After that, I went back to my cell and silently cried into a pillow just like I used to do as a child. My father beat me daily in those days. I stayed with him until he went to jail when I was seven years old. I was placed into fourteen different foster homes after that. I ran away so many times, they stopped chasing me."

"I'm so sorry to hear about all this," I said.

"Rev, I hated my father, but the night that I cried into that pillow I realized I'd become the man I despised so much."

A moment of silence overtook him as he collected his thoughts. He could no longer hold back his tears; they spilled over and ran down his cheeks because he was unable to contain all the pent-up emotions any longer.

"Like him, I don't have a single friend. I don't trust anyone. Like him, the women in my life are there because of the drugs I supply to them, or because they owe me money." Tears continued to stream as he asked me, "Will you pray for me"?

I knelt down on one knee in the midst of the filth, vomit, and garbage. He was still standing so I reached up to grab his hand. "Kneel with me," I said. He immediately kneeled and I asked him, "What would you like me to pray for"?

"For forgiveness and a whole new life," he answered. "Do you think it's all right to pray for that, Rev?"

"That's what men and women have been praying for from the time of Jesus," I responded and then waited for a minute or two of silence before I began to pray.

> Lord, hear our prayers. We cry out to you for grace and for the forgiveness of our sins. We seek a new direction in our lives—one that gives us hope, courage, and commitment. We seek to serve and love you. We offer up to you our hands, our hearts, and our souls—use them as you will. We're lonely, weak, and frightened. We need your love to hold us together. We ask you for the courage to move forward and the grace to make us new. Yes, we want to be born again into a new life. Amen.

He then embraced me and placed both his arms around me like a child holding his father. The sound of his crying created a holy silence in the space around all of us watching him at that time. Not a word was spoken as he got into his car and drove away.

It was three months before I saw him again, at the same place and at the same time. He looked different—more at ease and wearing average clothing. His chains and rings no longer adorned his neck and fingers.

"Rev," he said, "I just want to let you know that tomorrow I'll be flying to Africa to work in a missionary camp with orphan children. Will you pray for me? Will you pray that I'll have the courage to stay there and give my life to those children"?

This story took place five years ago. Recently I received a postcard from him. It read, "I'm still in Africa and have found a home here. I've found a place for my hands to do God's work. Thank you for the prayer you gave me that day on the street. I now pray for you every day. God bless."

Note: Talking about Christianity is cheap and easy. The words often flow from our lips without thought or consequence, as if they alone were enough to secure God's love. To walk the walk and have the courage to be, as Paul Tillich wrote in *The Courage to Be*, is a whole different matter. Only a few can go through the eye of that needle. A courageous Christian does not have an easy road to travel.

6

Cry of Lament

I cry out to you, O God, for the poor who are forgotten—for the men and women that I meet every day who are dying slowly and agonizingly on the street. I refer to the homeless, the sick, the mentally ill, and the addicted. O hear my prayers, my God. O hear my prayers.

THIS MORNING I STOPPED once again on Cormorant Street to find only one young man. Dan is his name. He's about thirty years old, and he's someone's son, perhaps someone's father. He could be you or me. He was sleeping in the fetal position on the hard, cold cement verandah of Pacifica Housing. A bit ironic, isn't it? Homeless, with just the clothes on his back, sleeping on the verandah of a downtown service provider whose mandate is housing the homeless.

When I woke him up, he was shivering from the cold. His face and hands were covered with large abrasions that were swollen and infected. His eyes were sunk into his face and one of them was black. He had dirty, stringy hair. His teeth were rotting out of his mouth; the few that remained were yellow and broken. As I sat beside him, his smell was very pungent. I offered him a cigarette, a coffee, and a new sleeping bag.

"I'm so damn cold and dirty! I need to get to Our Place for a hot shower," he moaned.

Section I: Muddy Water

"Get into your sleeping bag for now," I said. "It's only six in the morning. We're not open until nine. Try to get warm."

"It's six in the morning, Rev? Where am I"?

"You're on Cormorant Street," I said.

"Oh," he replied.

I left him there and walked about half a block, but there was something in my intuition, perhaps even a call from God, that caused me to turn around and go back to see him. He was surprised to see me again. I sat down amidst the filth around him and put both my hands on his right shoulder. Then I looked deeply into his bloodshot eyes. "God loves you," I said, as tears ran down my face. "It's hard for me to sit and watch you die a slow, painful death."

"Thank you, Rev. I know I'm dying, but it's good to know someone cares."

As I walked back to the car, I asked myself what more I might do, if I really cared. When I left him, I'd said these few words: "I pray that you'll start to dwell on life, not death."

Then I muttered a prayer to the heavens.

> Dear Lord, please be with Dan now, to walk with him and give him the courage to be. Amen.

7

The Victorias

I met Victoria the first month after I arrived in the city in 1992. She was wearing a high-turtleneck woolen sweater, and it was a hot July day. She always wore a turtleneck top. She never put on make-up, even lipstick. She was a volunteer washing dishes, picking up used cups, and wiping off tables. She was always there for her shift; she was one of those people we could count on.

Victoria was a quiet person. When I first asked her name, she responded timidly and then smiled. She was like an eight-year-old unsure of herself, and when she spoke, she was always seeking approval. "Did I do that right"? she'd ask. "Am I doing a good job? What more can I do"?

She was more than shy. Rather, she seemed uncomfortable in her own skin. It was as if she held a secret or a dark past that she did not wish to reveal. She'd suddenly have a mood swing. Someone would say something to her that upset her, and she would throw the towels or a cup she had in her hand, and then walk out of the drop-in center in tears. She'd come back a few days or a week later. Nothing was ever said about the incident. Although she never came in high from drug use, it was apparent to me that she was probably addicted to heroin or prescription drugs.

One day she told me that as a child, she was in her room when a fire broke out one night. She lost her mother, father, and younger brother to the fire. She got out through a window and was ok, at least physically.

I did not pay enough attention to her and never really got to know her well. My eyes were opened, however, five years later.

Section I: Muddy Water

Another woman came into the shelter on a frigid rainy night. She was very loud and scantily dressed to reveal her sexuality. I had seen her a few times on Government Street selling her wares. She was a well-known woman of the night. This was the first time I saw her in the center, although she may have been there a few times before.

"What in the fuck are you looking at"? were the first words out of her mouth to me. I didn't engage with her but walked the other way. She went into the washroom where the drug selling and injections often took place.

People outside the world of the street often question me as to why we would not just kick them out and bar them for life when they use drugs. When we open a drop-in center or a night shelter, we invite the street into our home. We invite them in with all their issues, their addictions, their mental health problems, and their experiences of loneliness. In our mission statement, one can read, "unconditional love in a nonjudgmental way." It was clearer than saying "living out the gospel in our lives."

Sandy, an excellent woman staff member, was working with me on the floor that day. I asked her if she'd check on the woman who was in the washroom, as she had been in there for around forty-five minutes. Without hesitation, Sandy went in to find her passed out in a bathroom stall. She'd fallen off the toilet and hit her head.

We called an ambulance, and Sandy went to the hospital with her. While at the hospital, Sandy got her real name. As soon as Sandy returned to the drop-in center, she told me that this woman had the exact name as our helpful volunteer Victoria L.

Two days later, Victoria, our volunteer, came in to do her shift. Sandy pulled her aside and told her about the woman she took to the hospital with the exact same name as her. Victoria broke into loud sobbing, so Sandy took her into her office.

Finally, Victoria gained her composure. "Sandy," she cried out. "I thought you knew to look at me—look into my eyes." Victoria was silent for a minute, and then with another outburst, she said, "She's my ghost. She is me, and I am her"!

Then she pushed Sandy aside and ran out of the drop-in center. We never saw either Victoria again, ghost or not. We heard that Victoria L. went to Vancouver, and she's probably living there today.

8

Emmanuel

THERE, LYING UNDER A tree on Dallas Road, was an older man covered by a simple grey blanket. He'd have been cold at night with the wind blowing off the Pacific Ocean. I often wonder how my homeless friends survive all night on the cold, wet ground. Every time I approach a person under a thin blanket in the winter, my mind takes me back many years to the time when I found a man who'd died of exposure on a cold winter night. I remember touching him. He felt hard and had purple and red blotches on his face.

However, as I touched this man, he turned his head towards me. I noticed his eyes first. They were beautiful and had no anger, fear, or bitterness in them. I felt the true presence of Christmas in his eyes. He was among the poorest outcasts of humanity: after thirty years of burying himself in a bottle, he was like Lazarus at our door. In his eyes and in the smile on his roughened face, I felt as if I was in the presence of Emmanuel.

If we open our eyes, we begin to see God appearing to us in the unexpected and the unwanted. He doesn't seem to show up in sparkling lights, wrapped gifts, or the blue boxes from Birks. If we look closely, we can see Jesus appearing in the suffering multitudes of our time.

As I touched his shoulder, he popped his head out from beneath the dirty blanket.

"Merry Christmas, Rev," were the first words out of his mouth. "I had a dream about my children last night. Both of them are adults now. I think about them often. They live in Wainwright, Alberta and are both married to military men."

"Have you ever tried calling them?" I asked.

"Rarely a day goes by without me thinking about calling them. But, hell," he continued, "I walked out of their lives when they were children, and it's best that I stay out of their lives right now."

"I think you should leave that decision up to them. Do you have their phone numbers?" I asked.

"I think a worker in Vancouver found them for me a few years ago, but I never did call," he replied.

After I handed him my cell phone, he looked at me briefly before beginning to rummage through his backpack, pulling out his phone book. He looked at me again and then began to dial a number listed in his open book. A minute later he closed down my cell and said, "Was it the right number? I don't know what it said, other than, 'Leave me a message.'"

The next day was Christmas Eve, and my phone was ringing repeatedly.

"Hello! You called my home yesterday. Can I help you?" the voice on the phone said.

"Where are you calling from?" I asked the Wainwright caller. "This is Reverend Allen Tysick; do you know Peter H."?

There was silence for a moment, then a broken voice answered, "Yes, he's my dad. Is he okay"?

"Yes, he's your dad, and he seems okay. Would you like to talk to him? It could be the best gift he could possibly have. He's not with me now, but if I find him and he's okay, will you call back at a time that's convenient for you"?

There was a lot of hesitation in her voice, but she suggested 5 p.m. that evening. I asked if her sister could be there as well.

I found Peter, and he talked to his daughters; they all spoke for the first time in years. As tears blurred his eyes, he looked at me. "They've decided that they want me for Christmas."

We agreed that I'd have him on the West Jet flight that leaves Victoria at 9:30 p.m., and they'd pick him up at the airport when he lands. I was able to bring him to Mark's clothing store and then to Rock Bay Landing for a shower and shave. We arrived at the airport at 7:30 p.m., and I watched him board the plane. I called his family to assure them that he was on the plane and would arrive on time.

Christmas is here. It's a time of celebration, Emmanuel. The homeless child had been wrapped in his rags.

As I drove home to my family that Christmas Eve, I thought, "It's one thing to hear the Christmas story, but it's another to actually get out there and live it."

9

Missing

10

Tell Him to Put His Shirt On

It was a bright sunny day in early July, 1998—a perfect day, in fact. What could possibly go wrong? I'd just passed the Whale Wall, and several members of my street family were sitting around just talking, laughing, or soaking up the sun. Several others were sitting there from all walks of life.

As I passed by the area, I thought, "This is one of the most beautiful cities in the world. Right now, it's at its best: rich and poor people, laborers, and government officials are all sitting together on a hill looking into the Inner Harbor, laughing and talking together."

In our human journey, certain specific stories are forged in our minds. Think of the stories locked in your own memories. The love of your mother or father, the day you received your first bike, the day you graduated, your first kiss, the birth of a child, the death of a loved one. Then there are other stories in our minds that are not as significant, but never forgotten.

This is one such story. Toughy was a First Nations woman who'd lived in Victoria all her life. Her ancestors all hailed from Ahousaht, a reserve on Flores Island, British Columbia. She was her own person who thought for herself, fought for herself, and lived as a liberated woman. One day, just after breaking up with her boyfriend, she said to me: "Men are like cigarette packages: good when you first open them up, but quickly emptied and easily discarded. When I throw them back onto the street, where I found them, the wind blows them away."

This story unfolds as the city explodes with flowers wafting sweet fragrances into the air. I'd left the Inner Harbor and was walking up Quadra

Tell Him to Put His Shirt On

Street. The bells of St. Andrew's Cathedral rang twelve times, announcing noon. Just then, I heard screaming from down the street. The farther I walked, the more intense the profane language and angry screams became, but I still couldn't see anything. The street holds its laughter, and this was one of those moments. When I reached North Park and Quadra, I realized that the explosive argument was coming from the parking lot of Sand's Funeral Home off North Park. As I approached, there in the center of the lot was Toughy, standing her ground against a young man of around her age. She had a black eye and fresh blood on her face.

About fifteen pedestrians had gathered, watching them battling one another. The young man was not too quick to respond to any of her many challenges. He was wise, for she was not to be underestimated. She accused him of stealing her welfare check, while he angrily denied it. The situation was intensifying as I arrived. Finally, the young man pulled his shirt off and threw it to the ground. Now bare-chested, he yelled out, "Come on, I'm going to kick the shit out of you"!

At that point, Toughy pulled her halter top down to her waist and, bare-chested as well, yelled, "We'll see who's going to kick the shit out of who"!

Just then, the police pulled into the parking lot. They knew them both well.

"Toughy," yelled an officer from his patrol car, "Put your top on."

She defiantly put both hands on her hips, pushed out her bare chest, and replied,

"Then tell him to put his shirt on."

The police officer yelled at the young man, "For God's sake, put your shirt on."

But just as he reached down to grab his shirt, Toughy gave him one of the best uppercuts I've ever seen. Then he landed unconscious on the ground. Looking over him, she said, "So, who'll kick the shit out of who"? She pulled her halter top up and walked off, listening to the applause of some of the women standing by.

The police picked him up off the ground. As he opened his eyes, he looked up at the policemen and said, "She's a damn tough woman, isn't she"?

This sent us all into fits of laughter. The streets are alive with laughter, love, anger, and revenge. Women's liberation thrives on the street because their very survival depends on it.

11

I'm Lonely

God of the poor, Lord of the weak, I cry out to you for your presence in our lives. Give me the strength, stamina, and wisdom to stand with the poorest of the poor—to walk with them and love them, always.

THIS MORNING, AS I walked the streets of Victoria, I met Linda J. on the corner of Pandora and Broad Streets. She was standing in front of one of the City Hall windows doing her make-up in the reflection there. I stopped and offered her a cigarette.

She said, "Oh, Reverend, I've been trying to look good again."

In the early morning light, I could see that her cheeks were pitted with sores, her eyes were bloodshot, and there were wrinkles all over her aging face.

"Rev, I really wish I could just die. I'm not sad about it because I've got nothing more to live for. You see, I've lost everything—that is, everything that's important to me. My children are long gone, and I haven't actually seen them for ten years. To tell you the truth, I don't even know where they are. But I do remember their birthdays: my son was born on February 27th, and my daughter was born on June 4th. He's now 19 and she's 16. God, I pray they're not making the same mistakes I made when I was young. Rev, I'm lonely. There's no one in my life and I have nothing except fucking narcotics."

Section I: Muddy Water

Then there was a silence, after which she started talking again.

"Just a fucking drug, that's all I've got. Last night I gave a man a blow job for $10. It's the only thing I know how to do well, but for a measly $10? I'm no longer a professional prostitute Rev, I'm just a fucking whore. I know I'm dying, but no one cares. I guess, you know—yeah, you know—I hate all men. They've all offered me salvation but, in fact, have taken the last drop of my blood to supply their habits. They've used me, abused me, and then thrown me away when I was no longer any use to them. In the beginning, they all said they loved me. But how can they love me when they don't love themselves? You know, Rev, I don't think I've ever really been loved, and the only people I've ever really loved were my children. I'm so lonely! Yet, there's something deep inside me that craves love. When someone says they love me, I want to believe it so much! I don't know why that is. Maybe it gives me some hope that maybe, this time, it'll happen—that someone will actually love me."

After a long pause, she continued, "Do you think God loves me? Do you think He'll love me when I die, or do you think He'll judge me? If He judges me, I'm guilty. No shit. You know it. No shit. That's what scares me the most. I'm afraid that, when I die, I'll go into the pits of hell. Fuck, it's just my luck to live in hell while alive and then have to spend an eternity in the burning hell of the afterlife."

Tears then began to flow. I wrapped my arms around her and after a time of comfort, said,

"Blessed are the poor, for yours is the Kingdom of God" (Luke 6:20 NKJV).

She looked at me. "Do you really believe that?" she asked.

"With all my heart and soul," I answered.

"Well, thanks for taking some time with me, Rev. You're all I have."

With those words, we parted. As we walked away from each other, I wondered if I'd ever see Linda again or if I'd ever even speak to her again and hold her in my arms. Those were the questions that haunted me as she disappeared into Centennial Square.

Five years after I wrote the above in my journal, I added: I stand over her grave site, as the coffin is lowered into the ground. And I repeat the words, "Blessed are the poor, for they shall inherit the Kingdom of God." I grabbed a handful of Mother Earth, creating a cross on the casket and committing her body to God: earth to earth, ashes to ashes, trusting in God's mercy and grace.

12

Just His Face

EARLY THIS MORNING, I was walking the streets of Victoria. I was in the Inner Harbor when I met a homeless man who is very religious. He's been living in our city for decades and is very intelligent. He's been called by God to live as a homeless man. He was sitting in his usual place, with legs crossed and eyes closed, but he was not asleep.

Just His Face

"Oh, it's you, Rev Al. I was just in prayer," he stated.

"How do you pray? What do you ask for?" I asked.

He hesitated and eventually said, "I just wait until I can see the face of Jesus. There are no words, no requests. I just look at His face in silence; nothing else is required. Faith," he said to me, "creates an open space in which the unexpected, the unpredictable, and often essential things in life can appear and become known. Faith is that space where miracles occur, new stories unfold, and new futures are born. But Rev, God has been silent for a while. I haven't heard His voice or seen His face in over a month. Would you pray for us all? Would you kneel beside me, hold my weak hands and offer up a prayer for all of us"?

I did as he asked. Kneeling beside him, I offered up this prayer:

> Lord, hold us, for we have no strength to save ourselves any longer. Lord, we cry out to be set free from all that denies us health, dignity, and respect. We cry out for love: to be loved, to offer love, and to find love. Oh God, we're so lonely, forgotten, unwanted, and desperate to find our place in the world. Walk with us in our darkness so we can find the light. Don't abandon us. Please don't remain silent any longer. Amen.

13

Wandering Spirit

I'VE HEARD THE LEGEND on the street many times before, over the years. It was always a little different each time it was told. It always had a new twist to it, but the essence of the story was never lost in the telling. I almost hesitate to write it down; it's as if putting it into written form would somehow cast the legend into stone, freezing it in history. I, however, am now an elder at age seventy-three, believing it's appropriate to ensure that this myth is not lost in time.

WANDERING SPIRIT: THE LEGEND

He lives on the streets of Vancouver, Victoria, and Seattle.

They say that the skin on his face is like the grooves in the bark of an old-growth tree, battered by the sun, wind, and rain. Pronounced more than most, his face's deep crevices sit on a weather-beaten skull.

No one knows where he came from or what tribe he calls home.

He is, however, definitely of First Nations ancestry. His nose, his eyes, and his face hold the pain and oppression of his people from ages past. His age is unknown. Some say he's as old as the trees themselves. Others say that he was blown here by the wind off the ocean and has saltwater running through his veins. No one can remember him coming to the city; it was as if he'd always been here from the beginning of time. Like the majestic mountains and the giant old-growth forests, time has no dominion over him; the legend is as old as the ancient ancestors.

He moves like the wind itself; it's said that he can be in several places on the same day at the same time. He's one with Mother Earth, subject to the laws of nature, not to the laws of man.

He's a very unassuming man, but when he speaks, his words reveal the wisdom of history. It's said that he always brings calmness, peace, and serenity with his words and his very presence, wherever he goes. He has an aura surrounding him that only the elders can see. It speaks of a world where we all live in unity and in respect for one another and for Mother Earth.

His name captures his essence: they call him Wandering Spirit. He's an artist on the street and is well-known by many. More important, he himself is Art, a canvas of time past and the constant reminder of what the future could be if we could just listen to the wind.

Section I: Muddy Water

The legend says that one day he attended a potlatch in Beecher Bay in or around 2010. Wandering Spirit loves to dance the dances of his ancestors. There at the potlatch, he and many others were dancing around a secret bonfire. He had a paddle in his hand that he'd carved, dancing with the paddle around the fire as it roared. Then suddenly, he moved into the fire and danced around in the flames. It's said that many saw the paddle catch fire, and finally, he was engulfed in flames. Then he walked out of the fire toward the ocean and disappeared. Some left the dance and ran to find him, but there were no footprints left behind.

The legend continues that he was seen that very day in Vancouver, Victoria, and Seattle, at around the same time as the potlatch in Beecher Bay. He has been seen many times since. Some say that they have even purchased art from him on his familiar corner of Hastings in Vancouver. Like the majestic mountains and the giant old-growth forests, time has no authority over him.

I have had two encounters with Wandering Spirit. He's well recognized by his black western hat, which bears a distinctive eagle feather. Underneath the hat is an American flag bandana draped around his head.

My office was on the second floor on the corner of Johnson and Quadra, directly across the street from the Island Health Sobering and Assessment Centre. One morning, I saw Wandering Spirit come out of that center. He saw me looking out the window. He gave me a big wave, but he walked on down the street and did not come in.

The stories about him continued, but my next encounter with him occurred years later.

There was what came to be known as the tin shack, across from Swan's pub and restaurant. It was put there by the late restaurant owner Michael Williams, and the homeless would sleep in it. Early one morning before the sun was up, I went to the tin shack to pick up a young man to take him to his appointment at Detox. The tin shack had only one door, with a wood stove and about six bunk beds. I stepped into the shack, and a large man I did not know jumped off a top bunk behind me with a hammer in his hand. He accused me of being a cop and threatened to drive the hammer through my head. Just then, the door opened behind him. He turned to see who it was, when a fist connected with his jaw, and he fell unconscious into my arms. It was dark, and all I could see was a black western hat with a distinctive eagle feather, leaving the shack.

When I got back to the van with the fellow that I was transporting to Detox, tied onto my van aerial was an American flag bandana.

Was it the ghost of Wandering Spirit who saved my life that night? Was it he who left me his bandana?

14

The Wilted Flower

"I shall be telling this with a sigh
Somewhere ages and ages hence:
Two roads diverged in a wood, and I—
I took the one less traveled by,
And that has made all the difference."

—Robert Frost's *The Road Not Taken*

My church ministry has frequently called me to travel on the road "less traveled by." I've seen the unbelievable cruelty of man. I've felt the pain and experienced the suffering of the weak and the vulnerable. Yes, I've seen Christ crucified.

One cold and wet early morning in November, as I walked the streets greeting the homeless by offering them coffee, cookies, and conversation, I heard someone moaning in pain.

Lying on the road between two cars was the woman nicknamed Cat, and she was obviously in agony.

"Thank God it's you, Rev. I thought it was them coming back to kill me."

She was in such great pain that I couldn't move her. I called an ambulance and, after a long wait, it arrived with two experienced paramedics attending. They got her safely to the Royal Jubilee Hospital. I followed them in my vehicle and spent the next six hours with her. It was there that she told me what had happened to her. Over our time together in the intensive care unit, we quickly developed a close relationship, as we shared our life stories with one another.

Earlier that night she was selling her services on the corner of Rock Bay and John streets. A car pulled up, and two men picked her up. That night she had no one watching her back: no one saw the men pick her up, and no one took down their car's license plate number. That meant that she was totally on her own. While they drove along, she agreed to service both men, and they all agreed on a price. After she'd completed her work, and before she got paid, one of the men opened the car door while the other shoved her out of the moving vehicle. Consequently, she suffered a broken arm and wrist, a badly dislocated shoulder, and got a nasty cut on her forehead that required five stitches.

As we waited for the X-ray results, she was rustling through her gym bag. After a long search, she finally found a flower. "This is for you," she said. "It's not much, but when I saw it, I thought of you."

As I held the wilted flower in my hand, I looked at her and said, "This flower means a lot to me, and I'm going to press it between the pages of my favorite book."

She responded by saying, "You saved my life today, and we now really know each other—you're a gift to us all."

I wouldn't have had the opportunity to get to know her, had I not been traveling the road "less traveled by."

15

Panhandling

O gracious and challenging Creator, as of November 1st, Our Place will begin panhandling for operating funds to raise $400,000 over the next eight weeks. Please help us.

On Monday I arrived at the drop-in center at 4:30 a.m. It'd been a miserable night with a torrential rainfall. About twenty-seven homeless people had been in the rain all night. They were awaiting my arrival, completely soaked. I then heard a heartfelt voice say,

"Hi, Reverend Al, we're all so glad to see you"!

After that, they all pushed by me with the only things they owned: shopping carts, bicycles, and back packs. I continued to hold the door open as they came in out of the rain, most of them with smiles as they passed by me.

"Thank you for my calling to the poor, dear God," I said in silent prayer.

Once inside, I went to the clothing room and emptied six or seven garbage bags full of donated used clothing onto the floor in front of them. My street family quickly rummaged through that dry clothing. The conversations, as they reached for and grabbed pieces of clothing, went something like this:

"Oh, this doesn't fit me. Here, it'll fit you." Or:

PANHANDLING

"This is nice and warm; you can have it. I have enough."

That is not what you'd expect from a group of people labeled homeless, addicted, alcoholic, and mentally ill. The truth is that I find more generosity, kindness, and love among the homeless than I find in most other areas of human endeavor. The poor are often the ones offering gifts to others.

As soon as some of them found clothing, they dropped their dirty, wet duds right there on the floor in front of them. Naked, they were in full view, and their bruises, cuts, and abscesses were fully exposed. What struck me, however, was the gauntness of their skeleton-like figures which were the blueprints of their journeys in life. Some asked for blankets and, cuddling up, fell asleep at the tables. Others put on the coffee and brought out peanut butter, jam, and bread. Many of them were extremely hungry. Have you ever watched someone who's very hungry eat? I have. They stuff the food into their mouths and haven't got the time to chew, so it splashes over their faces and their clothes. It's particularly disgusting for those with beards. This is not the hunger we all experience just before a meal, or even the hunger one experiences after not eating all day. No, I'm referring to the hunger one gets only after several days without food. Yes, it happens in Canada every day and more than we care to admit.

Section I: Muddy Water

As I took in the scene before me, my heart was pierced, as thoughts of my own full cupboard came to mind. Canned goods in abundance are in my home. My freezer's packed with foods of all descriptions. My pantry is filled with boxes of cereal, cookies, nachos, and a variety of other junk foods—not to mention the milk, juice, and cream. And let's not forget those Colombian coffee beans waiting to be ground for that first cup of coffee in the morning. My affluence is thrown into my face. Then I think of the many kitchens in this city, and of the unprecedented wealth of many of our citizens. Many, like me, have ample resources and go to the grocery store any time we want to buy food. I'm also aware of the food discarded today in restaurants, grocery outlets, department stores, and warehouses, and I know the Creator will not be pleased with our greed. I know that Mother Earth weeps since her bounty is plentiful, yet our greed is ever-increasing. You may be getting bored with my whining, but my tears are real, and my voice has been silent for long enough.

Now, let's get back to the story. I finally had time to sit with my street family in conversation and laughter—the thing that I enjoy most in my day. I walked out to the courtyard and sat with John Doer. John is a user and abuser of crystal meth. He had his thumb amputated just months earlier because of an infection that he didn't tend to. Both of his feet are now badly infected, while his life, unfortunately, is wrapped around the next fix. John told me that he was trying to see me all day yesterday, but I was out most of the day. I explained to him that I was panhandling: begging to keep the doors open.

Perhaps I should use more middle-class language. Yes, that would sound much more civilized, even clean. Yes, fundraising. Did you know that professional fundraisers belong to associations? They're accredited. Large, glossy, gold lettered plaques adorn their walls. I'm just a panhandler with no accreditation—nothing but an old-time church panhandler.

I sat down beside John to comfort him, but as happens so often, he had comforted me.

"How are you, Rev? You're looking tired," were the first words out of his mouth.

"Oh, I'm good," I assured him. Then, for some reason, I told him about my panhandling and my attempt to raise close to half a million dollars.

"Just one minute," he said. Then he began to empty his pockets, which contained old cigarette butts, crumpled, dirty, and ripped pieces of paper, and an old cookie. There, among the debris, was a single quarter.

Panhandling

"Here," he said as he handed me the quarter. "It's all I have, but it's a good kick start for your panhandling."

It was all he had, his last coin. The biblical story of the widows might come to mind. This one quarter will be the greatest gift I'll ever receive. I have that quarter today, taped to one of my journals with this story as a constant reminder. I am, in the end, just a panhandler that needs a kick start.

> Creator, you do challenge me, and yes, you do turn the world upside down.

16

A Sculpture

Creator God, you call me into the darkness, the void, the violence of humanity, and even into death itself. Surprisingly, it's there that I'm honored to be in your presence and feel your power.

It was 7:15 p.m., and I'd just arrived home. The phone rang; I answered it. It was Patches, a well-known woman of the night. Her voice was full of fear and trembling.

"Rev, Crystal's been badly beaten. She's in an alley on Johnson Street, and I think she's dead. I can't call the cops because they'll kill me too. God, I pray you'll come to her." With that, she slammed the phone down.

There are several alleys on Johnson Street, and I wouldn't know where to send the police if I did call them. To be truthful, some calls I pay no attention to, especially when I'm at home with my own family. But there was something in the urgency of her voice that came deeply from her heart, and I couldn't avoid that. I drove back into the city not knowing what or who I'd find. As I walked into many alleys, finally I could see her curled-up, naked body facing a wall of graffiti. The light of a wall lamp shone upon her. As I approached, she looked like a sculpture from a great artist, almost too beautiful to be real. But it was Crystal. I took my shirt off to cover her naked body, and then I put my fingers to her neck to feel her pulse. It was weak, but she was alive. As I moved her shoulders toward me, I called out her name. I could now see her swollen eyes and the crusty blood that had run down her face and covered her body. Finally, I heard a moan, so I put a bottle of water up to her mouth, called an ambulance, and began to pray.

A couple of police officers, who knew and respected her, arrived first. Just as one of them went to get some oxygen for her, the ambulance pulled up. Its siren was music to my ears. I then followed the ambulance to the hospital in my van and waited another four hours until the doctor told me she was going to be okay and that I could see her. She was awake when I went into her room.

"Reverend, I prayed that God would send me an angel to save my pitiful ass, and God sent you."

At that moment, I was but a vessel of God's ever-abiding love. The words that came from my mouth were from another source.

> God loves you so much. He gave his only begotten Son for your life. Thanks go to God, for he alone loves you with an ever-abiding love.

Section I: Muddy Water

She was in the hospital for three weeks, and from there she went to a women's treatment center. She's now working at a halfway home for battered women.

As I drove home from the hospital that night, I was close to tears. I realized I'd been standing on holy ground in the presence and power of God's love.

Thanks be to God. Amen.

17

Compassion and Humanity

Ron was in the doorway opposite an old antique store on Fort Street between Quadra and Blanshard. His reflection could be seen clearly in the store's window. The streets were dry that afternoon, because it hadn't rained for weeks. I could see him because the sun was on my back. He had to shut his eyes against the setting sun and was forced to breathe slowly and lean against a lamp post so that he wouldn't fall over. Since he couldn't hold back the sickness in his stomach, he soon began to vomit profusely. The blood in his stomach was quite evident in the puke that lay on the side of the road. He finally wiped his face with the arm of his dirty shirt and was off again, heading towards Douglas Street. I followed him, but I couldn't get across the street because of the traffic. Finally, the green light was in his favor, and he was about to cross Douglas Street when, suddenly, a police officer put his hand on the man's shoulder. By this time, I'd crossed the street. I was standing close by and could easily hear the conversation between the police officer and the older man.

"Hey, buddy! What are you up to"? the officer asked.

The older man raised his head to look at the officer, whose eyes were shaded by protective sunglasses. "I'm going for a drink," the old man growled.

"That's against the law," the officer quickly replied.

"Fuck you," the old man said, becoming more aggressive.

People walking by acted as though nothing was happening, as if they were all blind. For example, a group of young people passed by carrying

Section I: Muddy Water

placards reading, "Justice, Peace, and Freedom for All". Not even they noticed him.

Some disturbing questions then arose in my mind. Are we becoming blind to the world around us? Isn't anyone concerned about our brothers and sisters? Have we become like characters in Samuel Beckett's play *Waiting for Godot*, just sitting on the fence watching a world of suffering pass by, without getting involved?

Desmond Tutu is quoted in Brown's *Unexpected News*:

> If you're neutral in a situation of injustice, you've chosen the side of the oppressor. If an elephant has his foot on the tail of a mouse, and you say you're neutral, the mouse will not appreciate your neutrality.

I finally spoke up. "Anything I can do to help"?
"This is none of your affair, Reverend. Please move on," said the cop.
"Oh, but this is fully my affair, sir. You see, Ron's a member of my family. I've been following him for the last several blocks now. What's he done wrong, anyway"? I asked.

"He's been drinking in a public place, and that's against the law."

"He may have been drinking yesterday," I quickly replied. "But I just watched him get up from a doorway on Fort Street a few minutes ago, where he's been lying all morning."

Quickly, the officer responded, "He told me to fuck off."

Looking the old man in the face, I asked: "Ron, will you apologize to the officer for your language?" Ron raised his head again, looked at the officer, and said: "I'm sorry for telling you to fuck off."

Before the officer was able to respond, I interrupted. "Let me take care of this for you so that you can avoid all the paperwork."

"What will you do with him"? he asked.

"I'll take him to the hospital. He lost a lot of blood just a few minutes ago. You wouldn't want anything to happen to him in a cell, would you? You know what the media would do with that."

The officer leaned over and took off the cuffs. "He's yours," he stated. Then the officer helped me pick Ron up and said to him with some compassion, "You take care, Ron."

Ron responded, "I didn't think you cared."

The officer smiled. "Don't tell anybody."

Just for one brief minute, there wasn't a police officer or a homeless person standing there. There were just two men experiencing real humanity and feeling love and compassion for one another.

18

Cold Wind

It was one of the most profound statements I've ever heard—one that cuts into my heart as it exposes the pain of an addict. It wasn't said in the language of Shakespeare, Tolstoy, or Eliot. It was told from the only place such a statement can be told: from the deep pain of those who are homeless, hopeless, addicted, lonely, or lost.

Mike was an Inuit man from the Northwest Territories. His mother gave birth to him on a windy, cold day on the back of a snowmobile. When she was in her last trimester, she went out on a convoy with others from her village searching for caribou. When the labor pains became too frequent and the pain too intense, she motioned for the convoy to stop. Her mother-in-law knew what to do. The other snowmobiles surrounded her, acting as a weather barrier against the cold north wind that saw temperatures dip below minus 30 degrees. The mother-in-law quickly ordered the others to cover her with all the canvasses they had. A bearskin had been laid on her snowmobile, and that's where Mike was born. His mother named him Cold Wind. However, many years later, the Catholic Church renamed him Mike because they couldn't pronounce his Inuit name.

I've known him for about five years now. He's forty-seven years old, and his face is Inuit in structure with flat features, thin horizontal eyes, a strong jaw, and artistic wrinkles in his skin. Over the years, he shared the story of his birth and native name with me. When he spoke about his mother and his people, it was always with pride and strength that he remembered them.

Cold Wind

Most mornings I saw him sleeping in a filthy doorway in some alley, or on the veranda of the Victoria Gospel Church. This late November morning, I met him on Quadra Street on my way back to Our Place to help with the breakfast.

"Hi Mike, how are you?" I greeted him with a smile, not expecting the profound statement that followed. As he opened his eyes, he began to speak freely about his life.

"I'm forty-seven today and have lost a good wife and five adult children. I'm homeless and smell like a damn ashtray. At first, it was alcohol that drove me away from my family. But now I'm chasing rock cocaine because it's got a hold of my very balls. I'm no longer a man, just a piece of shit."

He put his head down and walked away, his statement piercing my inner being, challenging my understanding, engaging my heart, and leaving me speechless. Left alone on the street, his words were ringing in my ear, "I'm chasing the rock—it's got hold of my balls. I'm not a man, just a piece of shit."

I have no insights or words of wisdom to offer at this point. I have no theological answers either, and my mouth remains shut.

Is God silent as well?

19

Island Paradise

God, the beauty of your creation never ceases to amaze me, day in, and day out.

Today, particularly, as I drove into the city from Sooke, the bright red rays of the sun were beginning to peek brilliantly over the majestic Olympic Mountains. The sky and the ocean were alight with color. I pulled my car over, and I stepped out for a moment to be engulfed by the magnificent dawn. Standing there, I suddenly realized that I live on the most beautiful island in the world, thanks to God.

One hour later, I was in the city, driving the Our Place van as I delivered coffee and donuts to homeless people on the streets. Then the ugliness of the city presented itself to me. The first two men I stopped to greet were on Fort Street, both sleeping in one of the few doorways left without a steel gate blocking their entrances. They were sleeping right on the cold concrete, and one of them had nothing covering him. The other had a thin blanket.

"Reverend, do you have a sleeping bag?" one of the shivering men asked me.

"Not at the moment," I replied, "but I'll have one for you tomorrow morning for sure."

Then I put the box of donuts in front of them and poured some hot coffee for both of them. As I climbed back into the van, one of the men shouted:

"God bless you Reverend Al. God bless you."

Island Paradise

My next stop was on Johnson Street. Twelve men and five women gathered, all of them very grateful for the donuts and coffee. It was there that I heard that Chantal had been found dead, beaten to death in Beacon Hill Park. Before the morning was finished, I had seen fifty-six people. After that I thought:

> Oh my God, unlock the doors to some funding so that Our Place can open at 7 a.m. and offer my destitute, sick, and lonely people a good nutritious breakfast, a shower, and a bed to sleep in.

The glorious beauty of nature was in stark contrast to the city's reality of poverty, homelessness, sickness, and death on that day. I saw it all in a few hours.

Another prayer followed:

> God, give me strength. Give me the courage to walk with the poor and to be with them where they are. Continue to help me see the beauty of this island paradise, and give me the courage to articulate both the deep inequalities of the poor, and the changes needed to create an island of justice, for everyone.

SECTION II

Transformation:
Dealing with Death

20

Suicide

HE WAS ON HEROIN when he called. He was depressed and anxious, and suicide seemed to be his only option. It was 2 am and his voice brought fear into my heart.

"Rev, I called to say good-bye."
There was no doubt in my mind that this was a suicide call. I've had other calls like this, when the pain in their voice reaches out and grabs you like a drowning man clutching you as he goes down for the last time. The call invited me into his journey of suicide—it was the call I feared the most.
What could I say? How could I get him through his deep depression? I knew that I must keep him on the phone, keep him talking. I needed to listen closely and comment only when I had to. My task was to find those

Section II: Transformation: Dealing with Death

appropriate moments in the conversation when I might offer hope. I had to take this journey with him without judgment. At times, I could feel my heart pounding; there was no hope for him. We were now together in the darkest place of his suffering.

He's thirty-eight years old, and he's been addicted for eleven years. The addiction had gained complete control of his life like a dragon breathing fire on a chained-up vagabond. For him, suicide was the only answer. I could feel his pain, his loneliness. At times, I wished I could hang up, but his pain was so acute that I couldn't abandon him.

I knew that when a caller was full of anger, I could become the brunt of that rage. I also knew how important it was to only comment when necessary, and to make those comments short, clear, and truthful. He was the one who needed space, not me, the caregiver.

I'd talked to him many times before and knew that he had two children under the age of ten. I didn't want to take him deeper into his pain or to lay any guilt trips on the poor guy. I waited patiently, and when the moment was right, I asked him how his children were.

"They'll be better off without me," he cried.

I interrupted and said, "I'm not asking about *you*, I'm asking about *them*."

He then laughed a little and told me how great they were. Such conversations need to be listened to. At all costs I had to keep him talking.

The call lasted for two hours. In the end, he promised to see me the next day at Tim Horton's. I'd given him lots of time to vent, and he knew he'd been listened to. Thank God I was able to help him.

21

Oh Death, Where's Your Sting?

THE COLD DRIVING NIGHT rain had just stopped, and a heavy fog off the Pacific began to creep in. As I pulled the van up to Pandora and Quadra, he lay on the sidewalk outside the provincial Ministry of Social Development and Poverty Reduction office. Some hours before, he'd arrived at that location to pick up his monthly welfare cheque of $335.00. As I walked up to him, the stench of death was in the air as his body lay still and cold before me. At first, I just stood over him, trying to see if he was breathing. When I couldn't see any movement, I sat down next to him on the wet sidewalk. A young man—only in his twenties—he lay on that hard, cold concrete showing no signs of life. I called out his name and got no response. I slapped his face several times. Suddenly he gasped for air and tried to raise his head, but he just didn't have the strength to do that, so his head slammed back down onto the sidewalk. He was so weak that it was as if he had come back from the Spirit World to try to live again.

I wondered just how long he'd been lying there face down, with others walking right over him. Rats scurried in the low bushes nearby. One fat old rat ran right over his legs onto the street. Like the rats themselves, the young man was not wanted, just struggling to survive. The pest control people rid us of the rats. Politicians are paid to pass bylaws to get rid of young men like these. They live on the same street corners as the rats.

As he opened his eyes, he called out my name. "Rev, how long have you been here"?

"Not as long as you"! I replied.

Section II: Transformation: Dealing with Death

"Help me sit up," he asked. He then put his arm around my shoulder, and I managed to sit him up. As I moved him, I could see the pain of his aching body, but I could also see the mental anguish caused by his long history of suffering.

The light of the early morning was beginning to show its face as the fog lifted. I could see him more clearly now, and the rain of the night had seeped through and saturated his clothing. He was wet and shivering from the cold—or was he coming down from a drug high? Was the Dragon calling him again? At that point, he really noticed me for the first time.

"Rev, why did you stop? Why in the hell are you sitting here in this puddle with me"? Then he stopped talking and looked directly into my eyes. It was one of those rare times when one soul touches another: a sacred moment. Then he spoke again. "You should have walked over me like all the others do. I'm just not worthy of your time."

His words were so much the words of Jacob (Genesis 32:9–10, NKJV) that they touched me deep inside. Perhaps his words also reflected the way I've felt about myself at times. Tears flowed down my face. Seeing my pain and tears, he wiped my face with his hand and spoke again,

"You know what you are to me, Rev? You're like the power of fresh water on the lips of my thirsty soul." He wiped his head, where warm blood was running down his own face. Seeing the blood, he paraphrased 1

Oh Death, Where's Your Sting?

Corinthians 15:55, "'Oh death, where's your sting? Oh grave, where's your victory'? I'm dying. Why is God not covering me with grass and taking me from this world of pain? Rev, I'm looking forward to death. Just maybe I'll be like the thief who was next to Jesus on the cross, and Jesus will forgive me and invite me into His kingdom."

As he spoke, I asked God for the words that would give him hope and life again. Then, from my mouth came the old words from Scripture: "When I was a child, I spoke as a child, I understood as a child, I thought as a child; but when I became a man, I put away childish things... So now faith, hope, and love abide, these three; but the greatest of these is love" (1 Cor 13:11; 13:13 NKJV).

"The reason I sit here in this puddle with you is just to tell you this: you're loved unconditionally, and you're forgiven unconditionally. It's time for you to become a man, to set aside your childish ways, to stand up and be counted, and to accept the love of others."

He raised his head. A transformation of peace came over his face, as if his healing had begun. With tears still in his eyes, he asked me to help him to his feet. With all his strength and mine, we managed to get him standing. Looking at me once again, he asked, "Rev, did that happen?" and with those words, he collapsed into my arms, and I placed him once again in the dirty puddle beneath our feet.

I called out, "Are you alive"?

In a faint voice, with a bit of a laugh, he answered, "Yes, I'm still alive."

"You better not die on me today"! I yelled out.

He opened his eyes as wide as he could and answered, "Not today, sir, not today." He then took another deep gasp of air, crawled to his knees, grabbed both of my hands and pulled me to my knees. "I can't believe you're still here with me."

"We've both survived." I answered.

He replied, "Don't speak too soon—we're not on our feet yet"!

"I'll help you, and you help me. Let's get out of this damn puddle."

As we lifted each other to our feet, he repeated himself, "Oh death, where's your sting"?

I responded with the words of Edison (from thomasedison.org), "Many of life's failures are people who did not realize how close they were to success when they gave up."

I put him into the back seat of my van. He slept there until 4 pm. Then I took him to the A&W and fed him.

Section II: Transformation: Dealing with Death

"Where would you like me to get you to?" I asked.

He answered, "Where do you suggest"?

Without hesitation, I replied, "The sobering center, and in the morning, you can sign up for their Detoxification and Recovery Program."

"I knew I shouldn't have asked that question. I knew I'd get the truth," he said.

I replied, "I've got the easy path. I just suggested the direction, but only you can make the journey. It's not for the weak."

With that, he hugged me and said the familiar phrase of the street, "Take me to the sobering center"!

P.S. Dear reader, I wish I could add a happy ending to this story. But alas, he's just beginning his journey. Please hold him in your thoughts and prayers. Thank you.

22

Sombrio Beach

Bob was a lifetime alcoholic who was respected on the street because of his generosity and great sense of humor. He'd always share his bottle and had one beer in his backpack for the suffering alcoholic who might be shaking and in desperate need of a drink.

Back then, men on the streets traveled the city in packs like wolves, looking out for one another and watching each other's backs. Bob was the Alpha Wolf, a strong leader of the pack. He was from Newfoundland. When asked what brought him to Victoria, he laughed and said, "The police put me on the bus in the city of St. John's, Newfoundland, and told me not to look back. I ended up in Ottawa for years, but me, mother of God, I missed the ocean, so I put out my thumb on the Trans-Canada Highway and ended up in Victoria, where I settled down to be an upstanding citizen", and he laughed again.

Bob was a religious man born in the village of Ferryland, the heart of Newfoundland's Irish community. Although his grandfather and father were also born in Ferryland, Bob always said he was Irish. He believed in leprechauns, and he always wore a Saint Christopher medal around his neck, protecting him. Jesus was his Lord and Savior. He'd never crack open a bottle without spilling a few drops on the ground, remembering those who had passed on into the Spirit World.

When he stayed at the overnight shelter one night, we talked until dawn. He told me that he was "born again" one Sunday night at a Presbyterian church. "Now, mind you, my mother was half in the bag most of

Section II: Transformation: Dealing with Death

the time. She was an excellent Newfoundlander and could drink most men under the table. She had a good voice, and I can to this day remember her singing, 'What a friend we have in Jesus.' She always prayed that I would be saved by Jesus. I was at church with her one night as a young man, and the pastor called sinners to come to the altar and accept Jesus as their Lord and Savior. Rev, he looked right at me. I was sure he was directing his request at me. I knew that I was a sinner; that old *Playboy* in my backpack was a constant reminder. The congregation was standing, waving their arms in the air. So, I joined in with my arms in the air and danced up to the altar. The pastor slapped my forehead, and I fell to the ground. I was lifted up on angel wings, and I saw the face of Jesus. I was saved; praise the Lord! In spite of the spirit in the church that night, I could not wait until I got out of there to have a drink, of holy wine of course, and I'd invite Jesus to join me."

Bob lived with his friends on Sombrio Beach, British Columbia, and he found a home there. He'd sit carving on the beach, looking out at the waves, and offering up prayers to Jesus. For the first time in his life, he truly became part of a community.

His good friend died on Sombrio Beach. I had the funeral in Victoria at the Open Door. Bob found his way to the funeral that day, but for whatever reason, he never left Victoria and died there four years later.

A fight broke out on the street one night over a bottle of ginseng. He came to the defense of the man who was being beaten and was stabbed in the stomach with a dirty old knife, and infection set in.

I was the only one he had, and I was with him every day at the Jubilee Hospital in ICU for three days before he died. We took his ashes to Sombrio Beach a few days after his funeral, to spread his remains. Before doing so, I saw Barb. She and her family lived there back then. She was chopping wood for the winter.

Before I could speak, she said, "I sat with Bob on the beach for the last three days."

"I was with Bob at ICU for his last days in the hospital, and I'm here to spread his ashes," I replied.

Without hesitation, Barb said that Bob's ghost will join us.

Was it Bob's ghost sitting on the beach for the last three days? Did his spirit return to Sombrio Beach to say goodbye to the ocean and to the people that he loved? There are strange things done in the midday sun on Sombrio Beach, but the strangest tale told was when Bob's ghost joined us that day as we spread his ashes in the sea.

23

Free at Last

He made his mistakes.
He grew up in a home of privilege
And had all that money could provide.
His father taught him prudence,
His mother taught him peace.

His sister became a doctor,
His brother became a developer,
And he became a dropout,
Slower than the rest.
His mother loved them all,
His father had no time.

He stole his mother's jewelry,
His father's wallet in his hand,
He took his father's car and drove it fast.
He left the car in Sudbury,
His luck was running low,
His credit cards were canceled,
And he was out of dough.

He found himself in Montreal, drunk.

Free at Last

There he sold his mother's diamond
And many other of her things.
The waitress called a cab,
To the Greyhound he was taken.
Vancouver bound, sick and tired
He fell asleep, at the back of the bus.

He woke up in Calgary,
when rain was pouring down.
His backpack had been taken
And his wallet never found.
Now he lay on the ground,
As miserable as could be.

There is no happy ending.
The street became his home.
His father died in February,
His mother quickly followed
In the fall of that same year.

The RCMP told him of their passing;
His brother and sister went silent.
Not a postcard would they send him.
In their mind, he had already passed.

Section II: Transformation: Dealing with Death

He told me his story,
When I found him in a dirty alley.
He wrapped his arms around me
And I lifted him to his feet.
He told me he was loved by God
And that God had forgiven him.

He closed his eyes in peace that night
At the Jubilee.
I buried him at Hatley,
There was only me.

He grew up in privilege and died just like you and me.
In death we are all set free.

24

Fentanyl

ANOTHER ADRENALIN RUSH RECENTLY occurred in a young man who went down due to an overdose of fentanyl-laced heroin. He's only thirty-three years old and very lucky I was there with him at the time. I'm fast in emergencies and don't hesitate to act. I know what to do because I've had so much experience with these kinds of situations.

Section II: Transformation: Dealing with Death

First, I hit him in the ass with a shot of Naloxone. When he didn't respond, I gave him another dose in the neck. When that didn't work, I struck him twice in the heart. Suddenly, he took a deep breath and began to choke. I immediately put him on his side and drove my fist into his back *as hard as possible*. Then I inserted my finger into his mouth to ensure his tongue wouldn't obstruct his breath.

Life finally came back into his body. The ambulance arrived, and I went with him to the hospital. An emergency doctor told me he died for a few minutes, but the injections brought him back and saved his life.

This kind of work exhausts me now that I'm seventy-five years old. I sleep for only five hours a day, which has been a pattern throughout my whole life. When I hit the pillow, I'm asleep. After resting for a just few short hours, I wake up ready to run and face the day, whatever it holds.

Rescuing homeless people on fentanyl is the most exhausting work of all.

25

Give Me Grace

I ARRIVE AT THE Blanshard Street Tim Horton's to find a chaotic situation involving thirteen of my street family gathered there—eleven men and two women. It's 3:45 am, and I'm trying to write a few lines in my journal. However, three men are constantly talking to me about what happened the night before—or what their active imaginations *think* happened the night before.

One older man catches my attention in the disarray of the morning. I offer to buy him a coffee and he accepts, with a slight nod of his head. As I stand in line waiting for the coffee, strange thoughts are going through my head. What it is it about this man that pulls me toward him? What was his journey before we got together?

He looks so lonely, yet wise. Even though he's been beaten down by life, his inner strength is evident. His clothing is worn, ripped, and hanging from his body. His jeans are dirty, tattered, and twice the size he needs. But those pants are held up by a necktie which hangs loosely across his chest, drawing my attention to his oversized wardrobe and frail body. I sit across the table from him, on the other side of a booth. He raises his head slightly and acknowledges me. I feel like the flea on an elephant's back, which disturbs him from his loneliness for a moment.

Loneliness engulfs him like a cancer that's silently and agonizingly eating away his soul. No words are said. We sit in silence for a considerable length of time drinking our coffees, before I get up to leave.

SECTION II: TRANSFORMATION: DEALING WITH DEATH

Just then he grabs my arm firmly and speaks for the first time, "Rev, pray for me, and ask God to give me grace. Ask Him to take me from this suffering world, despite my past sins, failures, and shortcomings. Please, I beg you to pray that God will give me grace and accept me into the Spirit World."

Without hesitating, age-old words from the Book come forth from my mouth, "Blessed are the poor, for yours is the Kingdom of God" (Luke 6:20 NKJV).

"Yes, I'll pray for you and I'll pray for God's grace to descend upon you."

Tears run down the old man's face, and he lowers his head as he stands up. The air quickly fills with his putrid body odor as he moves away.

I think about smoke from church candles drifting towards heaven. Somehow, I know the odor from his dying body will be received with favor. This morning I'm in the presence of the trampled-down, defeated Christ—begging for the Father's grace.

"Abba, Father," he said. "All things are possible for you. Take this cup away from me; nevertheless, not what I will, but what you will" (Mark 14:36 NKJV).

26

Kaleidoscopic Eyes

I SAW HIS FACE, and he touched my spirit.

I've seen the eyes of a suffering Christ before in the faces of many homeless, addicted, and mentally ill people during my rounds. But this day was different. His kaleidoscopic eyes reached out and stripped my privilege away. I'd never be the same again.

I first saw him in the shadows of the night as he stepped toward the light. His beaten, wrinkled skin brought back many memories I've tried to suppress over the years. His smile was familiar too—it was the type that gave many of his First Nations ancestors hope and kept them alive when times were tough. That smile brought some of his ancestors back to life for me. I've buried many of them over the years.

All this man owned were the shirt on his back and the pants on his legs, and those clothes desperately needed to be washed. He took the last bit of change out of his pocket and purchased a coffee at Tim Horton's without saying a word. I watched him as he then gave the hot drink to another man sitting in a wheelchair outside the door.

This is the same man whose clothing was soiled with urine, the same man that many pass by with judgment and malice, and the same man that many do not wish to see, talk to, or smell. But the generosity and thoughtfulness of his ancestry are still alive in his veins, evident in his giving hands. The deep furrows in his face tell a story. They remind us of his ancestors' oppression, pain, and suffering.

This same man was later passed out on Douglas Street. I saw him from across the street as a female police officer kicked him. "Wake up and get your ass off the road, you drunken Indian," she yelled.

I crossed the street and said to her as I sat beside the man, "Please give this man some respect, officer. Your words pierce my heart. He's a hereditary chief and his ancestors owned *all* of this land just a few short years ago."

Just then, another officer pulled up in his squad car. "Get in," he said to his comrade. "The Rev. will take care of our friend."

As I sat beside him that day, he raised his head, and his eyes reached out and grabbed my heart, leaving a hole in it. His stare shook my very foundation. "Who am I beneath this human mask that I want the world to see? Who am I *inside*"? I asked myself.

Section II: Transformation: Dealing with Death

Then I noticed his calloused, cut, bent, and broken hands. They also told a story of the long journey he and his relatives have traveled in this land. When our eyes touched, I changed. Call it a conversion, a rebirth, or whatever you will. But the truth is that once I was drawn into his dark black eyes, I was transformed.

They say that a man's eyes are the windows to his soul. At that precise moment in time my soul was open. My weaknesses and sins were fully exposed. It was an uncomfortable place for me to be. This was a spiritual moment. I stood naked before him in body and in mind—an open book. None of my secrets could be hidden from him any longer.

Was this the same lonely man sitting in a coffee shop, not long ago? Was he the same man who'd lost his lover to the street and watched as white authorities took away their twin boys, never to be seen again? Was this the same broken-down man who could now hear the Great Spirit call out his name?

It felt as if a volcano had erupted inside me. My vulnerabilities, my weaknesses, my mistakes, my sins, and my wounds felt like molten red-hot lava running down my body, exposed for all to see. Could this man be the crucified Christ in front of me? If so, was I touched by him? Was it God's eyes that were engulfing my soul?

These questions tormented me. But then suddenly the spell was broken and the grip his eyes had on my soul loosened. I cannot forget his kaleidoscopic eyes—their suffering, their challenge and their transforming power.

We then embraced in a warm, sincere hug, acknowledging each other's pain.

Today I'm sitting in the Emergency Room at The Royal Jubilee Hospital with his 27-year-old son. He's also called "The Owl." He'll now take the same journey his father did and enter the Spirit World, joining all his ancestors—free at last.

We can look at his faults and blame them on his addictions. But I can't help but ask myself some questions. "What is our responsibility in all of this? Why can't we see what history has clearly revealed? Do we have enough courage to face our failures, our judgments, our hardened hearts, and our blind actions? Can we prostrate ourselves before God and ask for forgiveness? First Nations men and women are still dying in our social system today. How can we continue to stay silent?

We are still crucifying Christ every day.

27

Jim

JIM WAS FROM THE Songhees Nation. I've been honored, over the years, to call him a friend. He'd address me as a brother or a father, depending on the situation. His mother lived in a small home in Langford in which I'd been a guest many times, sitting at her kitchen table enjoying fresh bannock. If I found her son passed out downtown, I'd bring him to her home. He and his mother both had a good sense of humor. I remember one particular afternoon, after I'd brought him home for the third time in a week, when she looked up from eating her bannock and said, with a smile, "I swear, you go out and find Jim on the street just to come here and get another piece of bannock." Then we both laughed.

When I look back, there was always an air of spirituality around him. On more than one occasion, I've seen Jim and his friends share a cheap bottle of cooking wine they'd picked up from Chinatown, telling their stories. Suddenly, Jim would pull out his dog-eared Bible and begin to read:

"Love is patient, and love is kind. It does not envy. It does not boast and is not proud. It does not dishonor others; it is not self-seeking, it is not easily angered, it keeps no record of wrongs. Love does not delight in evil but rejoices with the truth. It always protects, always trusts, always hopes, always perseveres. Love never fails. (But where there are prophecies, they will cease; where there are tongues, they will be stilled; where there is knowledge, it will pass away.)" 1 Corinthians 13:4–8 (NIV).

Section II: Transformation: Dealing with Death

What always amazed me was the silence that overtook all who were present once he started to read. No one interrupted, and as soon as he'd finished, their conversations began once again without missing a beat. Nobody commented on the readings. Jim would just put the Book back into his pocket and start to pass the ginseng around again. When Jim was with them, no foul language was spoken because everyone respected his spirituality.

I only began to see this aspect of his character after being in many alleys with him over the years. For him, the bottle of ginseng was like a priest's bowl of holy water. He'd open the bottle, spill a few drops on the ground and say,

> Creator, we now remember all the men and woman who've gone before us into the Spirit World.

I couldn't help but wonder which prayer God would hear most empathetically: the one uttered by a priest draped in shining robes, or the one offered up by Jim in the alley.

Jim

Jim has since passed into the Spirit World. First Nations men and women still die at our white hands today. Can we be silent any longer about our shortcomings that contributed to his tragic life?

28

A Cry in the Night

My home phone rang several times before it woke me up, but eventually I answered it. On the other end of the line, a chilling cry could be heard.

"I just want to say goodbye. I've had enough of this dark, endless road. It's another lonely night for me and, in just two hours, it'll be Friday, April 3rd, 2020, which is a good day to die. I'm like the thieves who said nothing to Christ as they hung on the cross, awaiting death. Salvation isn't happening. The older I get, the more my past sins haunt me. Fuck, I've broken every one of the Ten Commandments. Rev, I only started praying when death was breaking me down. Right now, I'm remembering the prayer I learned on the street: 'God, if you get me out of this one, I'll give you my life.'

"I've got lots of excuses for my problems: the drunken father who beat me, the residential school staff that raped me, and the unjust court system that wrongly incarcerated me for five years. But I'm not blameless. I'm like Peter—I'd deny Christ three times for a bottle of booze. The Holy Book is in my back pack, and I read it every day. It never ceases to touch me in the heart. For example, the following verse always inspires me: 'Jesus saith unto him, I am the way, the truth, and the life: no man cometh unto the father, but by me'" (John 14:6 NKJV).

He then told me, "Only with the sting of death will I find rest."

I asked him if I could help, even just to talk together. But once again he replied by quoting scripture: "Take this cup away from me; nevertheless, not what I will, but what you will" (Mark 14:36 NKJV).

A Cry in the Night

    I wish I could give you all a Walt Disney ending, but alas, he took an overdose that very night. He died alone at the back of a filthy alley behind a dumpster and wasn't found for three days. Because Covid 19 was a concern, no public funeral was held. I was all alone with him at his Hatley grave site. As I lowered his casket into the ground, the following words came to me:

> May it be your will to remove this cup from my brother and give him a place at the table in the Kingdom of Heaven. He lived in hell on earth all his life; may he be given a seat on your right-hand side in paradise.

29

The Lone Wolf

MEL AND HIS TWIN sister spent their childhood at a Port Alberni Residential School that was the responsibility of the United Church of Canada. His sister died there, and neither he nor his parents were ever given the reason for her death.

I met him years later as he was panhandling. His lifetime choice of drug was alcohol, and he was always alone physically, but not spiritually, like a lone wolf that had left his pack. I believe he was meant to be born in another era. He was an *Indian warrior*, and it seemed like the dirt of Mother Earth ran through his bloodstream.

One miserable, rainy day in December, I approached him in James Bay when his back was up against a derelict chain-link fence. The worn-out leather jacket and bandanna wrapped around his head identified him. I sat down beside him, with my back against the fence as well. We sat in silence for the longest time. I felt I was invading his space, but then he moved both his hands, reached to the heavens, and asked the same age-old questions:

"Why are there rich and poor people?

Why have I suffered most of my life?

Why have I been homeless most of my life?

Why am I still frightened of the night and of the ghosts that haunt me?

Why doesn't God seem to help me"?

I was silent, the universe was silent, and Mother Earth was silent. That silence ripped a hole in the man's chest, and the pain and resentment of his history came spewing out of his mouth in violent profanities. He grabbed his backpack, which was the only thing he'd ever owned in his entire lifetime, and disappeared into the traffic. One could hear his voice long after he could no longer be seen.

He hanged himself in Beacon Hill Park two weeks later. His elusive mental battles were many. I buried him at Hatley Memorial Gardens, and when I did so, I was alone with his casket. It seemed proper for me to be alone because he'd been alone all his life. Now he was like a lone eagle flying in the sky, asking us all the difficult questions.

I come to you with his questions, knowing the answers are sparse unless your faith is deep. A few days after his burial, I walked up to the tree where he had hanged himself and knelt on the wet grass in silence, listening for God's still small voice in the void. It was then that I heard the voice in my ears:

"Why do you look for the living amongst the dead? Mel is living in the Spirit World now, you of little faith."

30

Red Feather

RED FEATHER WAS FIVE years old when he was taken from his family by the government system. The Sc'ianew (pronounced CHEA-nuh; Beecher Bay) First Nation is located 30 kilometers southwest of Victoria, British Columbia. The word "Sc'ianew" translates from the Klallam language as "the place of the big fish," indicating the richness of the sea life in the region that sustains the Sc'ianew and neighboring First Nation communities with food, shelter, medicine, and clothing.

He was a good-looking little boy with big dark eyes and a brilliant smile. Instead of going to a residential school, one of the workers took him home. He was never sent to school but became a slave to the family; they worked him day and night and fed him very little. Finally, when he was 14, he fled and lived on the street. I met him at 60 years old. He could not read or write and would ask me to read whatever he received from welfare.

Despite his childhood, the blood of his ancestors ran in his veins. He was generous and always had a big smile. I would wake him up in a doorway or find him sleeping at a bus stop. He'd immediately reach into his backpack to give me a chocolate bar or a book he had found. He had the welcoming and forgiving spirit of his ancestors. Most nights, he stayed in the sobering center. He always spoke highly of their staff and frequently brought them gifts. He was a chronic alcoholic, always having a beer on him. Most days he spent his time panhandling, but on especially cold or rainy days, he was in the drop-in center. I always knew he was there because I could hear his laughter.

Red Feather

One day Baby Girl invited him for a meal with others at her apartment in View Towers. Red Feather was the first to arrive and told Baby Girl he was not feeling well that day, suddenly collapsing onto the floor with a significant heart attack. Baby Girl called an ambulance; the paramedics saved his life that night. I have seen the paramedics save so many lives on the streets. They are all to be commended, often putting their lives on the line to save another.

The next day Red Feather called me, which was very unusual, asking if I'd come to the Whale Wall. It was named the Whale Wall because of the pod of orcas painted in 1987 on the side of the building. Adjacent to the green space (Reeson Park) at 1250 Wharf Street, it quickly became a geographic reference point and meeting place for city residents who'd sit on the grass of the hill enjoying summer drinking in the shade the wall provided. Recently, it has become a gathering place and encampment for homeless people.

I found Red Feather sitting alone on the rock retaining wall facing the Inner Harbor. I sat beside him in silence. He looked at me as only a First Nations person can—the look not only looks at you but also through you. Then he reached into his backpack and gave me a chocolate bar, which brought a smile to our faces.

"Father", he began, "you know I had a heart attack at Baby Girl's yesterday." (I'm often referred to as "Father" on the street, as a priest would

Section II: Transformation: Dealing with Death

be, out of respect.) "What you don't know is that when I hit the floor, I was transported onto a hillside, the traditional hillside of my people in Beecher Bay. I could see a large bonfire; its flames danced in the air. Then I began to see all my family and relatives that had passed into the Spirit World over the years. They were in full regalia, the traditional dress of the ancestors. They were all dancing in the old way around the fire. As they lifted their eyes, each looked directly at me sitting there. One by one they called me to the dance and beckoned me with the motion of one arm to join them as the dance continued. I got up and moved down the hill toward the fire; now I was so close that I could feel the heat of the big bonfire. Then someone came into Baby Girl's apartment. She screamed to get the hell out; the cops and ambulance were on their way up. I was immediately back at Baby Girl's, as the paramedics saved my life. Rev, do you think I was on the other side, in the Spirit World"?

Was this a hallucination of ghosts, or were they actual ghosts of his ancestors, inviting him into the Spirit World?

31

It's All a Plan

I walked into the hospital room, and the smell of decaying skin was pungent in the air. He was facing death, in his final stages of flesh-eating disease.

His name was Dwight, and I first met him in 2000 when he arrived from Winnipeg. I began to see him every morning on the corner of Pandora and Quadra doing what fondly became known as the Dwight shuffle. He simply moved from one foot to the other, constantly shifting his weight back and forth.

As one of the only black homeless men on the street, he quickly became very well known. Over the months, I came to know that his drug of choice was cocaine. He was both a user and a dealer of that particular drug. In spite of his lifestyle, he had honor and values, and he was generous. This earned him the distinction on the street of being *old school*. This refers to the way the street used to be when there was an honor code and honesty principles among the homeless and addicted.

Dwight was getting up in age, and the years living on the street, combined with his addictions, had not been kind to him. On one particular morning, that became very apparent to me. The time was 5:30 am, and it'd rained all night. As I walked across Blanshard Street, I saw him sleeping in the fetal position on the steps of the First Baptist Church on Pandora, without even a blanket covering him. As I approached, I saw that he wasn't moving and didn't do so even when I called out his name. I touched his shoulder several times before he finally woke up. Upon opening his eyes, he began shivering uncontrollably, with perspiration rolling down his face.

Finally, he spoke, saying, "I'm fucking scared, Rev."

I sat down beside him and held him in my arms. Even after he wrapped himself around me, I noticed that the shivering didn't stop. Breaking our embrace was not easy—it was as if he was holding onto life itself. I finally got him into the van with the help of my assistant, Ron.

At Our Place, I was able to put him into an empty room before calling the Cool Aid Health Clinic. Later, one of the street nurses came by to see him. Several hours later I checked on him, and he looked much better. A few days after that I was able to offer him permanent housing.

"Dwight, I've got a place for you at Our Place, and I'm only asking two things of you."

Looking directly at me he asked, "What are they, Rev"?

"First, keep your business outside the building, and second, keep it below the radar."

He reached out his hand, and we shook. I knew that his handshake would be his word. He moved in two days later and stayed with us for over a year, during which time his word proved to be good, and his health improved.

However, during the last month that he was there, he stayed in his room for days on end, not looking well. When we asked him how he was doing he'd say,

"I'm okay."

It's All a Plan

But he was *not* okay. He had flesh-eating disease and often just lay in bed in his own feces. Over a long weekend, we entered his room and called an ambulance. A week later it looked as if the hospital finally had his condition under control. Suddenly, however, his health worsened, and the doctor called to say that I should get in to see him immediately.

I've been in many hospital rooms and seen more people die than most, but I wasn't prepared to see what I was about to see.

There he lay: pink in color with barely any skin left on his body. Blood covered the bed, and he was bleeding from his face, neck, arms, and shoulders. The sheet covering his body and legs was bloody as well. I pulled up a chair beside him and put my hand on his head against his white curly hair, which was the only place where he was not bleeding. He opened his eyes and said,

"Rev, it's you. I've been praying that you'd come in. Look at me Rev—I've been black all my life, and now I'm going to die white." A smile came across his face. "It's all in my plan," he said. "I would rather have a white man go to hell than the black man that I was"!

Then he and I began to laugh and laugh. With my hand still on his head, he looked deep into my eyes and said,

"Thank you for the touch, Rev."

I then offered up a prayer:

> Lord, we trust that you are with us in life and in death and in life beyond life. Your presence is with us now in our friendship, in our laughter, and in our tears. You will never abandon us—in that we trust. Amen.

I lifted my head and looked at him again, with tears in my eyes. I took my hand off his head while his eyes stayed fixed on mine. Then he said,

"Thank you, Rev—you're okay for a white guy."

As I left the room, I knew I'd never see him alive again. His brother called me later that night and told me the news.

"Dwight just passed away peacefully," he said.

At his funeral, there were over 200 people attending, from all walks of life that Dwight had touched with his spirit. His sister and brother participated; they were both models in the fashion world. His sister stood and spoke, "Thank you all for attending. The turnout is overwhelming! My brother found a family here, and I will always thank you for that."

32

James

JAMES BELONGED TO THE Songhees Nation, and he was sixty-two years old. Not many generations ago, his family owned all the land we currently occupy in Victoria. However, today it's against the law for him to sit on a sidewalk downtown.

When he was five years old, he was taken from his family and placed into a United Church of Canada residential school in Port Alberni. His family didn't give their permission for this and didn't know where he went. He lost complete contact with his mother, father, and all his other family members, as well as his traditions and cultural heritage.

These stories are now familiar to us. In those schools, physical, psychological, and sexual abuses were prominent. James endured all this and began to sniff gasoline shortly after he arrived. He ran away at the age of thirteen and crawled into a bottle. Soon, the damage to his mind, liver, and general well-being was insurmountable.

Later on in life, he tried on many occasions to receive healing by going to treatment centers. He even held an AA medallion for six months of sobriety.

Unfortunately, two days ago I picked him up as he was face down on the sidewalk. He'd pissed his pants, and blood was running from his head as a result of his hard landing onto the sidewalk. The ambulance arrived and took him to the hospital, but he was pronounced dead on arrival.

The only family he ever had were street people. He called himself an apple: First Nations man on the outside and white man on the inside. His funeral was held at Our Place. At the service, JJ played the drums and Simon sang a song in James' mother tongue. He was buried at Ahousaht, and two eagles soared in the sky over his tomb to honor him there.

In life and in death, the Creator is with us. James is now with his ancestors in the Spirit World.

33

Obstacles

I BEGAN MY DAY praying for the courage and strength to deal with what I'd be facing today. It was 5:35 am, and I was sitting in my office looking out the window toward Pandora Avenue. I could see three people sleeping in the empty parking lot across the street.

"Here we are," I thought, "running transitional housing, a drop-in center, and a kitchen, yet the homeless still haunt me, pushing me to answer the more complex question: what next"?

Later that morning, I sat down for breakfast with the residents. Something compelled me to sit with Patricia. She was sitting alone, as far away from the other residents as she could.

"Can I sit with you and join you for breakfast"? I asked.

"Sure. Sit your old ass down there," she said.

She was not in good shape. It was easy for me to tell that she was struggling with her addiction. It didn't take long before she opened up to me.

"Oh, Reverend Al, I wish I were dead. Why must I go on living? I wish the whole fucking thing was over. I don't want to suffer anymore. Living on the streets or inside here doesn't make any difference for me. It's all the same: drugs, tricks, violence, threats, and collections. Cocaine rules my life. Suffering is around me wherever I look. I tried to help a girl late last night. I fought off her boyfriend who'd been dragging her by her hair down Douglas Street, so I threw a couple of big rocks at the bastard. He swatted me across the head with his hand, and I was on the ground, again. The next thing I knew, she was walking with him, away from me. I was lying in a pool of my own blood before someone called the paramedics. To us, they're 'the angels of the night.' As soon as I heard the ambulance, I had hopes for my future. Those hopes included getting into a detox program and getting clean for the first time in a year, once I got out of the hospital. Then, Our Place would hold a room for me, and I'd return with renewed strength and a commitment to move on with my life."

"Those are great plans, Pat," I said.

"Well," she replied, "all my plans fucking well fell apart. They told me I'd have to wait another three weeks before I got into any kind of treatment program. God, I hope I'm dead before then. Why doesn't God take me? Why can't I find rest? The truth is that fucking cocaine holds me completely under its power. I can't do it alone, Reverend, I can't do it alone. Pray for me, and ask him to take me today."

I looked into her eyes and said, "I believe in resurrection, in new life, new hope, and new possibilities."

"Oh, Rev, you're such a dreamer. You don't understand. I've never forgiven myself for letting my children go. Oh, I know it was the best thing for them, but holy fuck. Me, a mother, just letting them go with no idea where they'd end up, how they were going to be raised, or even whether they'd live or die. No, I don't want any more help. I want to die."

Section II: Transformation: Dealing with Death

"I can't let you go," I answered. "I'm going to be praying for you and advocating for you to get into detox now. I believe that a new life is possible for you."

"You pray then, Rev, and please ask God to listen to my prayers and answer me. I want to hear his voice."

P.S.: I worked hard advocating for her and got her in to see Dr. Nezil, who put her into detox immediately. Sometimes if a community works together, we can save lives.

34

The Dragon's Power

Creator, God of hope, here's my lament: I'm crying out for your grace and mercy.

THIS MORNING I ARRIVED at the Open Door at 4:30 am. As soon as I got there, I saw Shannon sleeping on the sidewalk outside the front door—in the center of a city that has extraordinary wealth. She'd consumed some crystal meth and couldn't stay awake, even standing up. I noticed a large, open abscess on her hand that was running with pus.

"Your hand looks horrible, Shannon. Let me take you to the hospital emergency before you lose it," I begged.

"Rev, I have to wait for my dealer. He said he'd meet me here. I need one more fix."

The powerful, evil dragon had her in his clutches. His fire was consuming her skin, her teeth, her mind, and even her soul. In the language of the street, this beast is known as *the Fucking Dragon*.

For all you puritans out there, please excuse the profanity, but it's the only way to describe the hold addictions have over my client family. I just have to sit there helplessly and watch so many of my friends being taken over by that dragon. His colors are like a rainbow and his powers are very seductive. He can lift vulnerable people up, as if on the wings of an angel, taking them above the clouds, above their pains, concerns, or real earthly issues. He'll flirt with you, lie, and then fondle your emotions. After that, he'll lie down with you and exert the full measure of his seductive powers.

SECTION II: TRANSFORMATION: DEALING WITH DEATH

Shannon was knocking on death's door. Her hair was falling out, she had scabs all over her face, and track marks were running up and down both her arms. Her hand was so infected that poison now ran through her blood. Yet, she yearned to sleep one more time with the dragon.

"Just one more hit," she said.

> God have mercy, God have grace, and please listen to my prayers of lament. Thank you. Amen.

35

The Flame That Consumes

Dear Creator,
You alone hold Mother Earth in your hands. You give the bear strength, the wolf wisdom, and the eagle sight. It's to you I turn with my wonderment and my requests. I ask you, Creator: can you enable me to see more clearly and understand more deeply the plight of the poor? I request that I be able to listen with sharper ears so that I can hear their cries better. I request that I be able to see with X-ray vision so that I can get beyond their physical appearances and fully understand their courage. I want to have them in my hands, my heart, and my mind.

I HADN'T SEEN DAN for over a year. The last time I saw him was at the Royal Jubilee Hospital. He was homeless at the time and had been diagnosed with cancer. He was also hopelessly addicted to heroin. With his doctor's help, we got him on a disability pension which allowed him to get a small bachelor apartment near Tillicum Mall. However, the distance from his new home to Our Place, combined with his deteriorating health, significantly reduced his ability to see me. In many ways, this isolation cut him off from the only community he had.

Dan is of First Nations descent, and he spent some of his childhood at a Port Alberni Residential School that was the responsibility of the United Church of Canada. My relationship with him goes back twelve years. However, I'd never really taken the time to listen to his story. I'd never held his

Section II: Transformation: Dealing with Death

pain. To tell the absolute truth, my communication with Dan was usually disciplinary. I often barred him from using the resources at Our Place for one or two days because of his actions.

I was on my way home after a very long day. It was 5:30 pm, and I was anxious to get out of the city, away from all the pain and constant requests from clients. I wanted to return to my family home and sanctuary in Sooke. But there he was, sitting on a rock barrier just past McDonald's on Pandora and Vancouver.

Dan looked like a skeleton draped with skin: his eyes sunken into his head, his face bones pronounced, his cheeks caved in from the loss of his teeth.

"Dan, it's been a long time. How are you"? I asked.

A big smile overtook his face. "Reverend Al," he replied, as he stood up slowly and hugged me tightly. "I love you, I love you, I love you."

After our embrace was over, we sat on the rock barrier together. Once we were sitting down, he held my hand and said,

"Rev, they've given me 'til Christmas to live. Cancer's spread all over my body. The treatments, the radiation, and the endless pills haven't helped."

There was then a period of silence as we stared into each other's eyes. It was only a fleeting moment, but over that time, I held Dan's pain. I felt his fear. I was burnt by the flame of cancer that consumes all he is.

He finally spoke up again. "But I am happier now than I've ever been in my life. Jesus Christ lives in me. Jesus came into my life the day the doctor told me it was over and that I'd die by Christmas. Over the past few years, Rev, I've prayed and tried to create a relationship with God. I remember my first prayer was after my diagnosis five years ago. Of course, after every cancer treatment, I was in prayer. But I hadn't truly given my life over to God. When the doctor told me that he didn't expect me to live until Christmas, we were in his office; it was pouring rain outside. I won't forget that day. I felt a chill coming over me as he told me, so I bowed my head, then and there, and said,

> Dear God, into your hands I commit my life.

Suddenly, I was warm. The feeling that came over me was like no other I've ever had. It was indeed a high—higher than I've ever experienced. Even a heroin high could not compete with the new high I experienced that day. The neat thing, Rev, is important: this high didn't go away. It's now with me all day and all night. It's not something I have to yearn for, steal for, or sell my body to get. No, this high's an eternal gift from God to me, the most unlikely. Don't get me wrong. I'm still on cancer medication and morphine for my pain. But, from that day on, I haven't felt the pain anymore."

He continued, "Oh, I still struggle with walking, my vision is piss-poor, I've got no appetite, and my blood count is dropping. But through all of that, I feel genuinely blessed for the first time in my life. I now know what it means when one says, 'I'm safe in the arms of Jesus.' It's funny Rev, I've tried to go to this church, perhaps a dozen times or so this past year, but I can't find the spirit there. Instead, I find my soul in the wind that moves the trees, the birds that take flight, and the mysteries hidden in every leaf and rock. When you bury me, Rev, I don't want any tears. Promise me you'll

Section II: Transformation: Dealing with Death

throw me a big party where there's lots of laughter. Remind everyone that I'll be with God, finally, safe in the arms of Jesus."

Dan's funeral was held on December 15, 2009, at his favorite spot: the Beacon Hill Park Petting Zoo. It was there that we told the story of his life. And we made sure to thank God for living in him.

SECTION III

Church / Street Ministry

36

The Gift of a Diamond

THE DAY BEGAN AS expected. It was a Wednesday, and I was sitting in the Tim Horton's on Hillside and Blanshard at 4 AM. In walked Rob, wearing bright clothing he'd salvaged from the Salvation Army thrift store and hand-sewn together. He also wore homemade, wraparound green plastic sunglasses and brightly painted yellow running shoes. His clothing looked like it'd been purchased from the world-renowned clothing designer Yves St. Laurent.

Rob's a rare person who sits on that thin line between genius and insanity, so he's always been difficult to understand. Still, over the years, employing a lot of patience and perseverance, I've had glimpses into both sides of his nature. That morning he stood at the coffee shop door, looking over his shoulder several times before entering. He immediately saw me and sat down at my table.

"Reverend," he said, "I found a treasure."

He had something in his hands that was hidden from view, creating an air of mystery. He then slowly and dramatically opened his hands, revealing a black pebble—something that you'd pick up off any roadside.

"It's a diamond, Rev. I found it on the steps of St. Andrew's Cathedral after sleeping there last night to get closer to God. Don't laugh—sometimes diamonds are black, and those are the ones that are the rarest."

"That's amazing," I said. "What are you going to do with it?"

Section III: Church / Street Ministry

"I'm not sure," he answered. "I need time to think about that." He then quickly got up from the table, looked over his shoulders, and disappeared into the darkness of the early morning.

If one takes time and has patience, insights into the complexities of mental illness can be obtained. It's not black and white, but different for every person. The best mental health professionals don't try to make homeless people conform to the values of our society. Their aim is to get the person back to who they really are. They understand that there are many degrees and types of mental illness. For example, some clients need institutional care, while others can walk our streets with minimal supervision.

Over time, I came to appreciate the rare genius embedded in Rob's insanity. He sees a world we miss. He can hold a grass seed in his hand and see its many future colors. He can feel its pain as it struggles, with unbelievable strength, to emerge through a crack in the street. He can mentally capture how a single blade of grass can become art as it miraculously bursts forth from a concrete world. Rob can even see the inner beauty in an old piece of clothing that's been discarded as garbage. He can unstitch that cloth and sew it to other colorful pieces of material to create a new and fashionable garment. He hears questioning voices in the night that we do not hear. Then he answers those questions to himself because he can't get to sleep.

"Are you lonely"? I ask him.

"How can I be lonely when everything in the night is alive? Most people can't see that life because they're sound asleep, but I'm not."

Late the following Sunday, he called me at home and said, "Rev, I just wanted to let you know that I put that diamond in the offering plate at the church this morning."

"That was an excellent idea, Rob," I answered, as a strange thought ran through my mind. The church had never given him anything—in fact, he was thrown out of it for speaking his mind during a service one morning. He'd symbolically given them precisely what they'd given him: nothing.

Rob ended the conversation by saying, "I'll see you tomorrow morning Reverend, at Tim Horton's."

37

Easter Story

AT EASTER TIME IN 2007, we conducted an outdoor Good Friday service for the homeless at Centennial Square next to City Hall, with a breakfast following. Three hundred people attended. The Our Place Board and many volunteers contributed and served that day.

As we were cleaning up, I received a call from Lawrence asking if I'd come to his room at the York rooming house and serve him communion there, as he couldn't get out of bed. The cigarette smoke, mold, and cockroaches were holding their ground against me as I climbed the stairs to his room. I knocked on the door.

"Let yourself in," he moaned.

As I opened his door, the smells of the place, combined with the smell of death, were almost too much for me to take. I was there to visit a dying man who'd called me on his cell phone an hour earlier. My heart was moved by the suffering, poverty, and loneliness of this person. His bloodshot eyes were sunk into his deeply lined face. They told the story of a man who carried his cross and was about to die.

It was Holy Week, and Christ was incarnate in this man and the many poor throughout the world, as they're still being crucified by the church and state today. This man's broken-down body, lonely spirit, and nearness to death is the ministry to which I'm called and to which I've given my life. He'd asked me to come to him while he journeyed from life to death, and to bring him communion in the process. Communion is an age-old religious sacrament of the Christian church. I came to break the bread and pour the wine with him.

Easter Story

The great honors I receive in this ministry are seldom pleasant or easy, and they've come with pain and personal sacrifice. Giving communion to Lawrence was one of the greatest honors I've received, for I felt that I was surrounded by holiness. Then I lifted his head from the pillow and served him the bread and the wine, saying the words that are so familiar to you and me from the United Church liturgy, "His body broken for you, His blood shed for you."

The man smiled. I've never seen a smile like that before. As I left, I asked him if I could call the ambulance and he answered clearly,

"It's over."

I respected his wish and left him to die alone, yet as I walked down the streets of this affluent city, Easter was mine.

38

Hear My Prayer

The words of scripture challenge, push, and haunt me, Creator God. I stand as an ordained minister of a church that's supposed to follow and live by your teachings. Both the Old and New Testaments make it clear that the poor are your children and the reason you sacrificed your only begotten Son. Yet, as I walk the streets of Victoria, I question the church's understanding of Scripture and our willingness to follow it.

At 4 a.m. I arrived in town. I walked the inner-city of Victoria, finding sixty or so homeless people sleeping in doorways, parks, and downtown graveyards. Those who were sleeping I walked by, and those who were awake I sat with. We talked about their plights, their struggles to find housing, and their sicknesses. I had no answers, no directions, no advice, and no help.

As the sun started to break over the majestic mountains, light hit the stained-glass windows of many of the magnificent structures we call churches, while the poor slept underneath their well-trimmed hedges. Inside those churches were empty gymnasiums, empty sanctuaries, and empty classrooms.

How can we possibly continue to allow this homelessness in our city of affluence? We could, if there was a will, end homelessness this very day.

As I was walking and reflecting on our selfishness, I found myself on Cormorant Street, where members of my street family were being moved along by the police and city cleaners. I sat with a seriously mentally ill man who was wearing a cheap plastic hospital bracelet that he'd received from Emergency the night before. Larry placed his head on my shoulder and whispered,

"Pray for me, Rev. Pray that God will receive me into his kingdom."

As I walked away, I offered up a prayer for myself, as well.

> Creator, if Larry isn't given a place in your kingdom, I don't wish to be there without him. Father, hear my prayer. Amen.

39

The Push

You push me into an arena that's not comfortable—certainly not safe, and decades away from the church's reality. Or do I push myself? It must be you, for I don't have the courage or the strength to push myself into the arenas of hell.

I WAS ON MY way home at 7:30 p.m. For some reason, let's call it "The Push," I turned down Cormorant Street and parked my car. I walked half a block to where there were twenty to twenty-five men and women sitting or lying on the sidewalk. Most of them were hooked on various drugs: cocaine, heroin, crystal meth, or crack. I came with my reputation and offered gifts of cigarettes and jelly beans, so I was welcomed, receiving many hugs and smiles.

I sat on the sidewalk, and while I was sitting there, the woman beside me offered me a blanket, which she placed around my shoulders. I felt like a priest receiving his vestments. After a while, I wasn't noticed. There, sitting by the wall just outside AVI Health and Community Services, I was just a person, not Rev Al anymore.

I was sitting in a scene that can only be accurately described as hell itself. I saw a man just a foot away from me filling a spoon with water and cocaine and then heating it with his lighter. He took a needle, drew up the cocaine, and casually leaned over and shoved the needle into the neck of the woman next to him. He injected her with the poison.

Then there was a woman just down from me, doing what we know as "the chicken": walking up and down the street and speaking to herself. Her arms and legs were moving sporadically around her. A fight broke out about half a block away between a man and woman. After a little while, another man got involved and I heard a loud voice,

"Where's my money"?

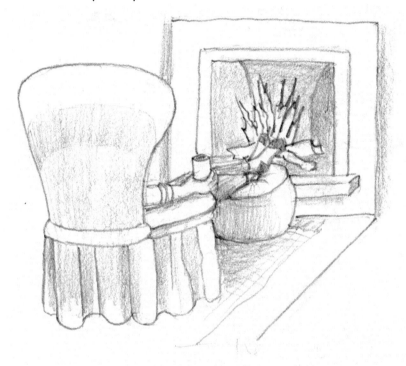

The woman continually screamed at the top of her lungs. No one seemed to notice the fight. It was as if only I could see it going on.

I then noticed that the woman who'd given me the blanket was sprawled out across the sidewalk, her feet hanging in the gutter. I took the blanket that she'd given me less than an hour earlier and put it over her cold, wet body. She was breathing. Her pulse was good. A car suddenly pulled up and three or four people immediately went to it. Money was passed, and one of the young girls climbed into the back seat and the car quickly raced off. Shortly after that, a police car passed. The officer looked out the window but didn't stop. By this time, my hips were getting cold from sitting on the concrete (arthritis, as you know). I got up off my ass with help from one of the fellows there, said goodbye, and got into my car and drove home.

Section III: Church / Street Ministry

Yes, I drove home to sit in front of a fireplace with a fresh cup of coffee in my hand as I reflected on the hell into which God called me and on the paradise in which I live.

Mary Hanes was born in Haynesville, eastern Ontario. She's my partner, a soulmate, a wife. Mary has given herself and our three children her life. Without her, I could not have given my life to the street. I arrived home late that night. She had a big smile, welcoming me with a fresh hot coffee and love in her eyes.

40

Exorcism

STRANGE THINGS CAN SOMETIMES happen during the rising of Victoria's early morning sun. One of the strangest involves an exorcism that I once performed.

It had been a "week from hell" involving two men, one young woman, and five fentanyl-laced-with-heroin overdoses. But thanks to the speed of many of the homeless people in town, since they administered Narcan, many lives were saved.

It was a Friday, and I was exhausted, but the week had not yet ended. My ministry would call me into strange, new, and dark directions. I received a morning call from the psychiatrist Dr. Michael Kovacs. He asked me if I'd stop by the social housing complex that accommodates mentally ill men and women, to visit a woman there he knew but couldn't help.

The housing complex was well staffed, and their residents were free to come and go at will. I was told by staff that the woman was possessed by "evil angels." Unfortunately, none of the traditional scientific or contemplative therapies were helping her. The doctor called me in as his last resort.

I'd previously been engaged with many on the street who swear they're possessed by the devil. I eventually became interested in this topic and began to study the subject of so-called black magic. I read as much as I could about the early Roman Catholic practice of exorcism. For example, a man told me in 1998 that evil spirits possessed him. Before he even stopped speaking to me, I asked him if he'd seen a doctor. He became furious—yelling at me and telling me I was just like all the others—not willing to listen to him. Two days later, he jumped off one of the balconies at the View Towers high rise in downtown Victoria and died.

After that, I intensified my study of exorcisms. I searched in hope of finding an answer within that dark world that the church had seemingly dismissed decades ago. I looked for a solution that might help a few outside the boxes of science, technology, rational thought, and medication. The more I studied and learned about exorcisms, the more dangerous they seemed to become, from an historical perspective.

In the 15th century, Catholic exorcists were both priestly and lay, since every Christian was considered to have the power to command demons and drive them out in the name of Christ. Those exorcists used the Order of Saint Benedict's ritual: "Vade retro satana," ("Step back, Satan").

Exorcism

Gabriele Amorth S.S.P. (1925–2016) was a famous Italian Catholic priest and exorcist of the Diocese of Rome who performed tens of thousands of exorcisms over his sixty-plus years as a modern-day priest. He used traditional rites and prayers, rather than the newer official ones that he found ineffective. I've continued to study and adapt the words of the *old* practices and rituals that suited my more liberal theological mind.

Amorth offered the following guidelines to those exercising the charism (spiritual gift) of exorcism. Any such person must be highly regarded for his prayer life, faith, acts of charity, and judgment. In addition, he must rely solely on the *Word of God* and the traditional prayers, be completely detached from monetary concerns, be profoundly humble, and treasure obscurity. "Heal the sick, cleanse the lepers, raise the dead, cast out demons. Freely you have received, freely give" (Matt 10:8 NKJV).

These days, drugs are often used to drive out what are called mental disturbances. Prescribed fentanyl is a powerful synthetic opioid that is similar to but fifty to one hundred times more potent than other drugs of its kind. Narcan is a naloxone hydrochloride injection used in known or suspected opioid overdoses. It's a thought-provoking crossover between clinical and street usage!

I've performed seven exorcisms over the years, with four women and three men. Here are the rules that I use for exorcisms so that we can remain comfortable during the processes.

1. Rule 1: The possessed person must trust the healer and the infinite power of God.
2. Rule 2: The practitioner must listen to, and believe in, the person's story.
3. Rule 3: The practitioner must be courageous and grounded in Christian faith.
4. Rule 4: The practitioner must go slowly and put their ego aside.
5. Rule 5: The possessed person's dwelling place must be as clean as possible.
6. Rule 6: The practitioner must bring:
    a. A bible, preferably blessed by a bishop or other church leader.
    b. A new rosary.
    c. A new, non-scented candle that's four inches in diameter.

Section III: Church / Street Ministry

    d. A Catholic cross (crucifix).

    e. A daily prayer book.

    f. Something to usher out the evil spirits, like an eagle wing or a prayer book.

7. Rule 7: All participants must have faith in the ritual.
8. Rule 8: Open as many windows and doors to the outside world as possible.

Let me bring you back to the woman Dr. Kovacs asked me to help. I visited the woman six times before she asked about an exorcism. Another staff member was with us at all times, as I slowly gained her trust. I told her that an exorcism was not someone doing something for her, rather it was her giving herself to God. When I told her she'd need to clean her apartment thoroughly, she engaged the available staff to help her so that it was spotless. Her participation was the fulcrum point of the exorcism that was needed. I'd given her a new bible with some marked passages and asked her to read them every day. I also left her with a candle to light as she said her prayers from the prayer book that I gave her. Many weeks later her belief in the power of God was strong enough to proceed with the exorcism.

The ritual was simple. I opened with a prayer asking that she be given strength. I took the Roman Catholic crucifix off the wall and handed it to her. She walked around every room in her one-bedroom apartment with the cross over her head saying,

"Begone in the name of Christ!"

I then read a few of the lines of scripture: "Away with you, Satan! For it is written, you shall worship the Lord your God, and him only you shall serve" (Matt 4:10 NKJV).

I then held the eagle wing, asked her to light the candle as I repudiated the demons, moving the wing through the air and saying,

> Begone, Satan, inventor, and master of all deceit, the enemy of our salvation. Be humble under the mighty hand of God; tremble and flee when we invoke the Holy Name at which those down below tremble. From the snares of the devil, deliver us, O Lord. That thy church may serve thee in peace and liberty, we ask thee to hear us.

We then walked through every room, ushering the evil spirits out her front door, ensuring that all the outside doors were open so that the evil spirits could leave the building.

After the exorcism, she cried out, "I am set free, and they are gone. Jesus is my Lord."

After the exorcism, I was physically and mentally exhausted. I had to pull over on the highway and have a nap before continuing homeward. It was the same with each of the exorcisms I performed.

The doctor told me he hadn't seen her in such peace for over a month.

There's a strict spiritual exercise that one must continue to do every day to strengthen the spiritual muscles, so that they can protect the person against the return of the evil spirits. For six weeks after the exorcism, she was to read Matthew 4:10 and then light the candle and say the Lord's Prayer. She maintained her practice for about two months before the spirits returned.

What is this demonic force? The scientific world would say it is a mental disorder, brought about by addiction or prescription medications. After all the years I've spent investigating these questions, I'm not certain. I am certain, however, that we need to pay much more attention to the world outside science, electric shock, meditation, and incarceration. The answers will vary and be numerous. Demonic forces, black magic, casted spells, and evil spirits have been documented throughout history.

Will I do an exorcism ever again? Every time I get close to the demonic, I get burned. If, however, God calls on me to do others, I'd be obedient.

Warning: Do not attempt an exorcism unless you have years of training; it can consume you.

41

Judgment

WHEN THE CALL CAME in, it was 2:30 p.m. on Mother's Day. My whole family was over for lunch; we had a barbecue going in the backyard and were enjoying some precious time together. My wife Mary answered the call and passed the phone to me because the woman on the other end seemed distressed.

All I got to say was, "Hi, it's Rev Al," before she burst out screaming,

"Why are there so many bums on the street? Why the hell don't they stop taking drugs and alcohol and abstain from those toxins, like we do"?

As it happens, I live with that question. It's at the core of my being, my heart, my mind, and my soul. Most of my contemporaries don't realize that my father lived on the street. They don't realize that when they ask hateful, malicious questions, they're asking about my current street family. I've lived with them my whole life and have come to love them as they love me. They live in my heart—they're *my* children, *my* family.

The angry woman on the phone that afternoon was not the first person to ask me this question with judgment, anger, fear, and hate in her voice. So, I'll attempt to answer her question with a true story that helped me grow my spiritual understanding. You'll need to be courageous, non-judgmental, and unbiased to fully comprehend the significance of this tale. I hope it'll help you transform your understanding of yourself.

Tonto was a Cree from Piapot, an Indigenous First Nation in Saskatchewan. Tonto's mother and father left their reservation at the age of thirteen and fourteen respectively and moved to Edmonton. Tonto was born off-reservation when his father was in jail and his mother was an alcoholic. His actual birthplace was a dirty motel room off the Trans-Canada Highway. No doctors or nurses attended the birth.

School was not in the cards for Tonto because his family moved too often, to avoid paying rent. But the Ministry of Family and Children's Services took him away from his parents and placed him in a foster home after his mother left him in a car for twelve hours on a hot July day.

When his foster mother beat him with a paddle, he ran away, never to return. He was fourteen years old at the time. However, the foster family never reported him missing for over a year so that they could continue collecting the income.

For the next while, Tonto slept in doorways with the rats and ate out of garbage cans. At the tender age of fifteen, he was picked up by the police for stealing a chocolate bar. The court system placed him in a youth detention center, where he was frequently beaten and raped.

Years later, when he was eighteen, he was sleeping in an abandoned alley when an older man molested him. A fight ensued, but the perpetrator was much bigger than Tonto and kicked him when he was lying face down on the ground. But the young man fought back, using his feet. One of his

Section III: Church / Street Ministry

kicks caught the old man by surprise and knocked him down. When he landed on the concrete, his head split wide open, and he died instantly, splashing blood everywhere. Tonto was quickly arrested and pronounced guilty in what he claims was a kangaroo court. For that, he served seven years in an adult prison.

This is where his education began. He worked out, lifted weights, and fought the toughest men in prison, until he gained their respect. Upon release, he returned to the street, which was the only life he really knew. Once again, he was living in doorways and winter shelters, and eating whatever he could grab from garbage cans or discarded boxes of Kentucky Fried Chicken.

For a few years, Tonto was top dog on the street. No one dared tangle with him because life had made him tough and brutal. He was in and out of jail but, when free, he always returned to the streets of Victoria. One night he beat up a man he accused of stealing money from him. The victim was so badly injured that he had to be admitted to the hospital. I know that because I visited him there. When I saw his battered body, I judged Tonto harshly and carried resentment towards him. But, at the time, I knew only one side of the story.

I met Tonto again in December, 1996, during Victoria's great snowstorm. I'd just opened up an emergency shelter that weekend and was inviting all the homeless people out of the snow and the cold. Tonto came into the shelter late that night, drunk and angry. Despite that, he lay down and fell asleep.

However, in the morning, he started fighting with the man on the mat next to him, accusing him of stealing his money. I then got between both of them and before long, I was actually fighting with Tonto. I was thirty years younger but did have a weight advantage of about 150 pounds. Remember, I also had a *street life* background. In street fights there are no rules and no honor. You fight to stay alive, and the best man walks away. The loser might end up unconscious, or dead. Finally, I got control of the situation, threw him onto the ground and sat on his chest so he couldn't move. Then I looked him directly in the face and said,

"You can tell me this is over, or I'll hold you here until the police show up—the choice is yours."

"That's fair enough," he answered. "It's over. Now will you take your fat ass off my chest so I can breathe"?

JUDGMENT

We both laughed. it was over. In those days, after a good fight, the two survivors often became friends, as we did. Over the years, late at night, he'd tell me his story about what brought him to the shelter that night, and what kept him living on the street.

He could be your son or daughter, your father or husband. His life was the product of the Ministry of Family and Children's Services, the Victoria Police Department, and the federal prison system. He was dealt a bad hand at birth and didn't have a chance to live a meaningful life.

People like Tonto stay on the street because there's nowhere else for them to go. Why in the hell did he keep on drinking? *He did it to kill the pain.* Now the big question: why isn't he just like us? If you're courageous enough and honest enough, ask yourself what decisions you'd have made in his shoes. Perhaps that question will make you see that he's more like us than we care to admit.

"Judge not, that you be not judged. For with what judgment you judge, you will be judged; and with the measure you use, it will be measured back to you. And why do you look at the speck in your brother's eye, but do not consider the plank in your own eye" (Matt 7:1–3 NKJV)?

42

The Tea Room

It was already 11:30 a.m. My day had started at 3:00 a.m., and I'd finally found time to stop at a tea room and have a pot of tea, hoping to have a few minutes of quiet.

It'd been one of those hectic mornings where I'd given out warm blankets and served coffee and doughnuts to eighty-two homeless individuals. I'd already taken one young man to Emergency due to an abscess on his leg, and I'd helped another move some bags into his new apartment. I'd given out five sleeping bags to people who needed them. I spent time talking with a young man whose father had died two days before. It was Easter week, and the images of Christ carrying the cross through the streets towards Golgotha were vivid in my mind.

I really needed to be alone for a moment and stop to catch my breath. However, the minute I sat down with my pot of tea, a homeless man dressed in rags sat down right next to me and called out loudly,

"Reverend, isn't it"?

The table server then raised her head and told me to take the man outside. He was well known at that establishment for his deranged outbursts. So, I stood up slowly, put a smile on my face, and left my pot of tea to get cold at the table. Then I offered the man a cigarette and suggested we go out to the road. He complied and followed me onto the street. As I stepped onto the sidewalk, I knew that the street was more my home than a tearoom could ever be.

"How can I help you"? I asked.

The Tea Room

He didn't hesitate to raise his voice. "You're a Reverend, aren't you? What kind of Reverend are you anyway"?

We'd only bumped into one another briefly over the years, but I knew he was a recluse. When I'd approached him in the past, his wishes were always clear. "Leave me be," would be his only words.

However, I could tell by his tone of voice that it wouldn't be wise to desert him now. We'd never actually sat down and had a good talk before this. To sit with someone in their pain is the greatest gift one can give the other.

"I'm a Reverend ordained by the United Church of Canada," I answered.

Before I could say another word, he interrupted, "Can you take care of my spiritual needs"?

He then narrowed his judgmental eyes and peered into my soul. I was immediately drawn into his darkness. His sorrowful, drooping, baggy eyes intensified into a ghostly stare. It was a haunting, lonely, frightening place for me to stand, but I couldn't avoid him at that point. His eyes opened the door to my naked soul.

"You *do* know something about God, don't you?" he asked, waiting silently for my answer.

Section III: Church / Street Ministry

"Yes, I've studied theology most of my life. That means I've inquired into subjects like God, faith, hope, and love."

He abruptly responded in a demanding voice, "Then let me ask you something. I've been hearing God's voice my whole life. But what do you think he's trying to tell me"? He was asking the question but not really wanting my answer.

There's something about the designation "Reverend" that's been a curse rather than a blessing on the street. Many homeless people think that I hold a toolbox full of all life's answers, such as God's purpose for pain, suffering, death, heaven, and hell. At that particular moment, I wished I could have just slipped back into the tearoom and placed my hands around my warm pot of tea. I felt deeply disappointed that this engagement had disturbed my peace and tranquility.

Just then, the morning sunlight bounced off a nearby tree and caught the man's wrinkled brow. His white hair was stained with nicotine and his golden-brown eyes were deeply buried in a suffering old face. He wasn't seeking an answer—he just needed someone to stand in the abyss with him.

My call to minister to the poor came from God when I was very young. I was the most unlikely candidate to be called to the cloth because I'd grown up on the streets of Ottawa myself. My mother had raised my sisters and me on a welfare budget. I was very human and made lots of mistakes in those days. I still make mistakes!

The Christian religion is a human institution. Historical sins made by all the Christian churches were created by an endless search for wealth and power. Nevertheless, at its heart, the teachings of Christ are transformational. Faith can teach a person how to live meaningfully and treat others compassionately. I can honestly say that the bible I've carried all my life is now carrying me. I've always been a square peg in the round hole of clerical rectitude. From my earliest days as a follower of Christ, I understood that the calling was never going to be easy. It was never an invitation into a life of affluence and privilege. It's a calling that takes us into the suffering of life where courage is required to stand in the darkness that lives in the mind of every man and woman. For me, it was always understood as a sacred sacrifice of my flesh, body, blood, and soul. I've always understood the call: *literally* a willingness to lay down my life, if need be, for the poorest of the poor. So, at this moment, the beam of sunlight brought me back to my calling.

As the old man cried out, "What has God's voice been calling me to do"?, I was still deeply entangled in the gaze of this older man's soul. As tears ran down his face, he raised my arm up to the sky. Calling out, he said, "God's voice is soft and gentle. One must listen very closely to hear It. He talks to me about the end of my journey; he tells me that my suffering is ending. His voice assures me that I'm loved."

He then slowly showed me his hands like an innocent child would show his mother. They were the hands of a dumpster diver: muscular, dry, dirty, and infected. His palms had holes in them just as though he'd been nailed to a cross.

Without thinking, I blurted out, "Have you gone to a clinic? Has a doctor looked at your hands"?

His yellowed eyes flashed wide open and gave me a look of dismay and disappointment—a look that pierced my heart. He then closed them and, in doing so, closed the doorway to his naked soul. Still weeping, he then became much more aggressive, shouting at the top of his lungs,

"You're so disappointing, you're not who you say you are; you don't understand after all. You're blind to the love of God. You're as blind as the rest of them"!

Then he suddenly turned his body away from me and swung his arms through the air, punching the wall of the teahouse with so much strength that his knuckles bled. That swing could have landed on me! I stood by, silently watching him almost disappear into the traffic. I knew that I'd interrupted a confession buried deep in his heart: the story that he wished to finally share. It was as if I was standing on holy ground in front of the burning bush. But unlike Moses, I was unwilling to take off my shoes and engulf myself in the heat. He was about half a block away when he stopped, turned around, and shouted at the top of his lungs,

"I thought you'd be brave."

I'd committed the cardinal sin in outreach: refusing to listen. Rather, I'd jumped in with my own thoughts and conclusions. Perhaps I wasn't brave enough. Maybe I'd found an escape hatch and used it. All he really wanted was for me to be silent and walk into the darkness of his soul with him. But being weak, I ran the other way. If only I'd had the *courage to be*. This important teaching is about my own lack of faith, hope, and love. I only hope that you, dear reader, can learn from my mistakes.

Two years later, this homeless man died under the Johnson Street Bridge. I was the only one there when he was buried. Social services paid

SECTION III: CHURCH / STREET MINISTRY

for his funeral, but no one knew his name, social insurance number, or identity. No headstone was ever laid.

I named him, "Hot Tea."

43

Harley's Untimely Death

BARRY MORRIS HAD SENT me an email. He is a lifetime friend who became a mentor. I had asked for his counsel a few days before, and he sent me the theological thought I needed. Barry is a theologian. Like me, he's struggled with theology at the deepest levels throughout his ministry at the Longhouse in Vancouver.

I was doing my usual walkabout, waking up the homeless, giving them coffee, water, and doughnuts, but most importantly I was profoundly present with them. As Barry had said in his email, my presence has been the heartbeat of my ministry on the street.

This morning I arrived at 4:30 a.m., and I could hear crying across the street on the corner of Pandora and Quadra. Ironically, the addicts, the sick, and the forgotten sleep there every night on the veranda of the Ministry of Housing and Social Development. They arrive after dark. They are unwanted and feared by many, but they congregate there and find a place where they're welcomed by the others in similar circumstances. However, the scene is one of chaos, filth, and death. The church and society look upon them with disgust and judgment, offering them only the police and ambulances.

As I approached them, I heard loud sobbing. Screams of anguish were coming from Rachel, who was weeping for her friend, Harley. Her crying wouldn't stop, and she refused to be comforted, because Harley had died, and she was the only family Rachel had. Harley had been pushed in front of a bus by two men who'd been drinking all night at a local bar. Seeing me, she became angrier, screaming,

Section III: Church / Street Ministry

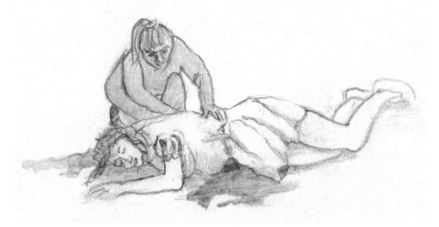

"Why did God take her? He should have taken me. I am so close to death I have tasted it. Why did he not take me"?

I sat beside her in the hurricane of her pain and listened; sometimes, silence is all I have to offer.

Many of her friends grabbed me, weeping and needing comfort. One question lingered on their minds: *How could God let this happen?*

I continued to minister to them all morning, listening to their anger and watching their tears.

"Where is God in all of this"? They kept asking. I didn't give them any answers because the same question was on my mind.

But I was also wondering, where are *we* in all this poverty we've created?

44

Mother Mary Chamunda

A READING FROM LUKE'S scripture came to mind when I first discovered a man and a woman sleeping in a sordid alley. They were tucked away under a staircase, and the smell of garbage, human waste, and vomit was in the air.

"He has shown strength with his arm; he has scattered the proud in the imagination of their hearts. He has put down the mighty from their thrones and exalted the lowly. He has filled the hungry with good things and the rich he has sent away empty" (Luke 1:51–53 NKJV).

They lay naked beneath a dirty blanket they'd found. The beauty of their naked bodies intertwined and formed a scene of artistic grandeur. Their clothing was neatly piled beside them. He was in the fetal position, his head on a rock that was covered with some rags. She was behind him in the same position; her perfect young face lay on the small of his back and her hand sat lovingly on his shoulder. It was a picture of contrasts: a beautiful couple lying in a horrible alley.

Years ago, I came across a book by Shusaku Endo entitled *Deep River*. In it, I was introduced to the goddess Chamunda of India, who displayed all the suffering of the Indian people. She's contracted the poison of the cobras and other venomous snakes. Despite all her suffering, her image causes gasps for breath as she offers milk to mankind from her shriveled breast. Her body evokes the history of India. Chamunda is India's Mary of the poor. She's not pure or refined like the Christian Mary. She doesn't wear a crown, doesn't have rings on her fingers, and isn't robed in blue silk embroidered with gold thread. On the contrary, she's an ugly woman, worn with age and groaning under the weight of her pain.

Section III: Church / Street Ministry

When Beth, the young woman I was looking at in that alley, looked directly into my eyes, I thought of Mother Chamunda. This is the Mary I've come to know in my ministry. She's the Mary who knew hunger, thirst, and loneliness, and she's the Mary who could sing from her heart, "He has filled the hungry with good things, and the rich he has sent away empty."

Beth had no inhibition as she grabbed her clothing and started to get dressed when she saw me. I turned my head.

"Have we embarrassed you with our naked bodies"? she asked.

He spoke up, and said, "Let the man off the hook."

Then they both laughed. I learned later that he'd studied to be a Jesuit priest, but when they met at a church service, it was love at first sight, and they ran away together and had been running ever since.

I couldn't imagine that their kind of beauty could emerge from an alley that smelled like the sewer rats that were running freely about. It was a scene worthy of being painted by da Vinci because it involved the faith of a Jesuit and the beauty of a Cleopatra.

> My God, my God, you appeared to me today in the most unlikely place!

45

Burning Eyes

This week I received a call from the Dandelion Society asking me if I could help a homeless woman who was suffering from a mental illness. I found her sitting on a bench near the Wax Museum along the Inner Harbor.

I find mental illness clients very intriguing. They remind me of black holes; when I muster up the courage to get close enough to someone suffering mental illness, I stand on unstable ground. They usually just can't see any light outside the darkness surrounding their reality. Some function quite well throughout their entire lives, while others must be confined to an institution that has professional staff who can administer medications. But I don't think institutions are the answer. We desperately need more understanding and resources on the street to support and *be present with* those who need our care.

This particular woman has been hospitalized many times. She functions quite well despite periodic outbursts and occasional meltdowns. On this day, she was clear and logical: a woman of wisdom and someone worth listening to. It's important to remember that everyone has good days and bad days, not just those who suffer from mental illnesses. As I sat beside her, she immediately broke her baguette in half and handed me my portion. That act reminded me of Sister Margo Power, my spiritual mentor. Many years ago, when I lived in Montreal, she once said to me,

"You'll always know the poor. They're the ones with no shoes who offer you gifts."

Section III: Church / Street Ministry

A sacred moment of silence overtook us as I sat down beside her. We both ate the *bread of life*: the baguette that she shared. No priest's communion wafer could have possibly brought me into that holy moment.

The words of the Holy Book came to mind, "He multiplied the loaves and the fishes, and he fed the people" (paraphrased from Matt 14:13–21 and John 6:1–14 NKJV).

This is not the end of my story. The bread that she shared with me not only satisfied my hunger but also touched my heart. Faith questions engulfed my conscious mind. I had affluence and privilege, while she had nothing but a loaf of bread. And yet she offered half of it to me. The bread she gave me that day nurtured my soul. It came from the poorest among us: a woman judged by society as worthless because of a mental illness that was not her fault. She was always in danger of being put away, unsupported, and out of our sight. When we finished the bread, she held my hand, then stared at me with burning eyes.

"Why did you become a minister"? she asked me.

I was asked that same question during my ordination forty years earlier. I was sitting in a cold room with six other professionals, being asked questions the officials thought were the most profound spiritual queries that could ever be asked. But they were dry, academic, and theoretical. I remember thinking,

"On this dull day the professionals are asking their hollow questions in the halls of McGill. I feel like we're outside the world rather than in it."

That day when they asked me, "Why do you want to become ordained and serve the church?", they were surprised and bewildered when I answered,

"I'm not called to serve the church. I'm called to serve the poor. Unlike the other students here, who come from families of wealth, I come from a background of poverty. Indeed, I'm the most unlikely candidate to be called to the cloth."

Immediately another graduating student spoke out, "Do you realize you're going to have to be obedient to church policies and doctrine"?

Then a woman that I'd never met before spoke up: "The actual church statement is, 'a candidate for the ministry must be obedient to God's will and follow church policy and doctrine.'"

An awkward moment of silence fell upon us before we moved on. I never did answer the question as we turned to other mundane, boring, secular questions. In fact, it was the only real theological question that I was asked.

"Why did you become a minister"?

Now, forty years later, I'm being asked that question again. Not by academics, priests, or politicians, but by the poorest among us. Not in a cold room on a dreary day, but on a bench in Victoria's Inner Harbor on the Pacific Ocean. A poor, homeless woman is inviting the world to hear my answer. As she asks the question, she is searching my soul. Silence captured this holy moment. The only sounds were the ocean waves hitting hard rocks on the shoreline as her burning eyes cried out for my answer.

Then a question came to my mind: just how big is my ego, my sense of self? I felt her eyes igniting me like the flaming eruption of a volcano. The lava melted my ego completely and brought me to the truth: I'm less than a grain of sand in this vast universe. Finally, I was able to speak.

"My mother was a poor woman. We ate the crumbs that fell from the tables of rich men. We were expected to be thankful for the rotten food given to us by local food banks, and grateful for the empty prayers offered

Section III: Church / Street Ministry

up for the poor at every mass. We were expected to be in awe of the wine and the wafer offered from the carved communion table adorned with gold candle holders and a large crass statue of Jesus hanging there as a symbol of salvation—all of this while blocks away children went to bed hungry."

I continued, "Most people look for God as someone who is found in a specific place like a church, synagogue, or temple. I encounter our Lord in you. We meet the Lord every time we meet the other, especially those who are in dire need, the least among us, the addicted, the mentally afflicted, or the lonely. There I have found God."

She then tightened her grip on my hand and interrupted my homily. "Why did you become a minister"?

I responded by saying, "I became a minster to meet the Lord in you and to see him in your burning eyes."

She was silent for a moment before letting my hand go and starting to laugh. "Well then, the Lord is hungry. How about getting some poutine and a bottle of wine to wash it down"?

After we ate the poutine together, and just before we parted ways, she said, "Rev, don't tell them I'm the Lord. They'll lock me up for that one and throw away the key."

46

The Prayer

MY SPIRITUAL MENTOR TAUGHT me: "The power of prayer can move mountains." I dedicate this story to her.

> Creator, I prayed to you in the early morning light. I prayed to you as the City Hall clock struck noon. I prayed that you'd spare the life of a dying man I found lying under a bush in Victoria.

Later that night, I was asked to open a Board meeting in prayer. On my way home, I stopped by the hospital at 10:35 p.m. and stood by the man's bedside, praying over him again, until early the following day. I was the closest person he had left. His doctor told me they'd done all they could for him, and death was soon to follow. The doctor asked my permission to pull the plug. I agreed and then sat holding the man's hand in prayer as he began his journey into the Spirit World.

Then I asked God some questions:

1. Where are you, God?
2. Why do You remain silent?
3. Are my prayers being cast into the void?
4. Are you too old to listen any longer?
5. Are my ancestors wrong?
6. Is the Book that I carry empty after all?

SECTION III: CHURCH / STREET MINISTRY

Oh, I could fall back on the text of the familiar hymn to say, "In his death, he's now 'safe in the arms of Jesus.'"

Well, that answer's not good enough for me any longer. I left the hospital at 4:30 a.m., headed to open up Our Place for the day. As I arrived, I asked God to give me the strength for another day.

When I arrived, Larry G. was lying in a ditch: dope-sick, filthy-dirty and smelling pungently of urine. I picked him up, carried him into my office and put him into a sleeping bag on the floor. The scent of his body quickly filled the air, but he was now safe, for the moment. I prayed over him as he slept.

> Great Spirit, have compassion—see to Larry's tears, come to him.
> Take pity on this, your child.

The Prayer

Later that day, I went into the men's washroom at the drop-in center, and the first thing I saw was Larry crunched up on cocaine. I first noticed his large eyes, then I saw the needle in his right hand, injecting his neck with poisonous cocaine. Yet, in his eyes, I saw the suffering Christ.

Over a lifetime, I've been looking for, and praying to, the omnipotent God that the church and seminary taught me about.

> But I didn't expect to see you, oh great God, in the eyes of the junkies, the weak, the sick, and the scared, along with this dying man.

God hasn't let me down. He has responded to all my prayers. I now know that God has never been silent. But He walks and cries with the poor because they're oppressed. He's crucified every time one of them dies.

Have my prayers been answered? No, not in the traditional way, but yes—only at a depth that goes well beyond my understanding. The prayers are collected and put into a melting pot of justice with the prayers of others, so that our closed eyes might someday be opened, and we might then hear the call to pick up the cross and follow Jesus all the way to Golgotha, if necessary.

47

Shopping Cart

THEY'D ASKED ME TO preach at a nearby church. I'd attended the early morning service and had approximately an hour and a half before the next service began. So, I decided to go for a coffee at Tim Horton's on Douglas Street.

After finishing the coffee, I headed toward Blanshard Street, which led me to the back of Staples, where their large garbage bins are located. A dumpster there was covered with graffiti and had its lid open. I noticed a lumpy bright blue sleeping bag inside one of the garbage bins. I looked into the sleeping bag and found old Joe there, about fifty-five years of age, snoring away. I woke him up and asked him what in the hell he was doing in the dumpster.

"I was getting out of the damn cold and having a good sleep until you woke me up, you fool," he said. "Why else would I be lying in here"? I reminded him that just a year earlier one of our family members was killed by sleeping in a dumpster. He answered, "Hell, it's Sunday, Rev. They don't pick up garbage on Sunday. You should realize it's Sunday, Rev"!

By this time, he'd crawled out of the dumpster. I could see that he was dirty and had pissed his pants during the night. He was also cold and wet. I suggested that I take him to Our Place so that he could get a hot shower and some clean clothes.

"Do you mean that?" he asked.

"Of course," I replied.

Shopping Cart

He then went around the corner and brought forth a shopping cart, full to overflowing. We emptied the shopping cart to put his belongings into my van, and then we tied the cart to the roof of my vehicle and drove to Our Place. I emptied the van quickly and left him with the staff there. I was quick to speed off, because by this time I was running late for the second service at the church.

Minutes later I'd put on a black Geneva gown and was with the priest and vicar in a procession. I was handed a large, shiny, perfect gold cross and told to lead the procession while the congregation sang.

"Holy, holy, holy, Lord God Almighty," they chanted as the sun beamed through the many stained-glass windows. A gold chalice was brought to the communion table along with the gold plates that would soon be used to collect our offerings. Several candles were glowing in the morning light, held high by gold candleholders. We all continued to sing.

I felt as if I was in another world. Just moments before, I'd been standing near a dumpster digging out old clothes for a homeless friend, and now a new Geneva gown was hanging from my shoulders as the church's pipe organ played and the congregation sang.

Section III: Church / Street Ministry

Was I in another world? Or was I in a church that wished to ignore the world outside its walls? It was just like other churches—not comfortable welcoming guys like Joe. The congregants were somehow blind to the gospel messages about serving the poor, blind to the fact that God's children were being forced to sleep in bushes, dumpsters, doorways, and alleys, and blind to the reality that our gospel calls us to *do so much more*. The real Christian message calls for us to give up our own lives to save others, if need be.

48

My Argument

I SIMPLY ARGUE
That the cross be
Raised again at the
Center of the marketplace
As well

Section III: Church / Street Ministry

As on the steeple of the church.
I am reinstating the claim
That Jesus was not crucified
In a cathedral between two candles, but on a cross
Between two thieves, on the town garbage heap, on a
Crossroad so cosmopolitan that they had to write
His title in Hebrew, Latin, and Greek.
It was the kind of place in which
Cynics talk smut,
Thieves curse, and
Soldiers gamble.
Because that is where he died, and
That is what his death is about.
And this is where Christians
Should be and this is what
Christians should be about.

SECTION IV

Articles and Speeches

49

Do You Have Your Heart On?

ONE DAY, A WELL-MEANING, born-again evangelical woman showed up at our drop-in center. She was fundamental in her faith and always somewhat of a concern to me. She had good intentions and a gentle disposition. That day she showed up with small paper heart stickers and was offering them to everyone. She put them on their chests; they said, "Jesus Loves You."

At the end of the day, Angus, a 6-foot-tall First Nations man sleeping in the corner, finally woke up.

She noticed him and immediately said, in a loud voice for all to hear, "Angus, you haven't got a heart on"!

He smiled devilishly and replied, "Well, that could be arranged."

The whole drop-in center burst out in laughter, and the woman turned two shades of red.

Another day an old-time Newfoundlander came in with a dozen roses, knelt down on one knee and asked the same woman, as loudly as he could, if she would marry him. "We both have been single all our lives, so let's not miss this opportunity. I will even take a bath," he continued. At that, she and all around broke out in laughter.

Another day, a box of dresses came in—the type you see in a show. Two of the women convinced her to join them in a can-can dance for all at the center that day. Everyone joined in the song and laughter.

She came into the office one day and said, "I came here to save the souls for Jesus, and they saved me. I came to teach them about God's love, and they gave me God's love. I came to volunteer very seriously, with a mission to lead them to the Lord, and they led me to laugh and taught me how to step out of my comfort zone to find God in places I'd never have looked. One of the women asked me last week, 'Do you really think your shit doesn't stink? Do you think you really have the answers to all our problems? Do you think the answers are easy and simple? Your head is up your ass. You're no better than we are.'"

Transformational change can happen in the mind and soul of every individual if we're willing to listen to others, and if we are willing to change. The woman with the paper hearts touched many, and the men and women at the drop-in center touched her. Together they moved charity to justice; salvation to transformation.

50

Betty

THERE ARE MANY STORIES told, but few are about the volunteers and donors who make it all possible.

This story is about a long-time donor who also did a significant amount of volunteering. I first met Betty fifteen years ago, after her husband passed away, and her children had long since left to live in various other locations across the country. She had become an *empty nester*. She had met her husband when she was only sixteen years old, and they got married two years later. After that, they lived in a house in Oak Bay for fifty years. I met her after a church service at Oak Bay United. She told me at the coffee hour that she was lonely and looking for something meaningful to do with her life. I suggested that she volunteer at the drop-in center.

The following Monday, she washed dishes and served our family there. She was a gift from God, fitting in so well—a natural at work. Her years of successful parenting gave her a PhD in human relationships and negotiations. She became like a mother to all; our street family fell in love with her very quickly. She was more than a volunteer; she was like an unpaid staff member. She never missed a day and was always willing to do something extra, if wanted.

Unfortunately, arthritis and other health-related problems put an end to her volunteering with us. She lived for several more years alone, with some home support. Every month, however, she'd send a generous donation to us with a card offering prayers and hopes for our family, volunteers, and staff.

Section IV: Articles and Speeches

Recently, I received another card from her, telling me that she wasn't able to give as she had in the past, and that she was forced to go into a nursing home due to deteriorating health. But she was still offering her prayers and thoughts to those on the streets. She's truly an unsung hero to the homeless and destitute of Victoria.

There are many other donors who, like Betty, have given their hearts, souls, and resources to Our Place over the years. Without them, we'd never be able to continue our ministry.

To Betty and all of you out there who support our work: your gifts are received with gratitude and thanks. You are our heartbeat of unconditional love in a non-judgmental way. Thank you!

51

The Unknown Strangers

Do you believe in the miracle of Christmas? I believe it because I witness modern-day miracles every day on the streets of Victoria. Let me share such a miracle with you.

Section IV: Articles and Speeches

His name is Ed. I've known him for ten years and he's been homeless for the last four. He sleeps in a doorway on the corner of Douglas and Courtney Streets. He's an old man, one of those fellows who've survived on the streets against all odds. I don't want to paint a picture of an angel, and he wouldn't want me to either. He carries a long-time addiction to alcohol. His face is pathetic, weather beaten, and wrinkled. But his brilliant blue eyes could pierce the hardest of hearts. He's been sick recently, perhaps the beginning of pneumonia. I've tried to locate a place for him but have so far been unsuccessful due to his lack of financial resources.

Then, on a crisp, cold night with the stars visible even within the city, some strangers approached Ed and offered to rent him an apartment. They said they'd pay for it. Ed accepted it and is living there now. Apparently, the strangers even furnished the apartment.

These are the miracles of Christmas: visitors from the east following the star and offering gifts to the needy. This city is full of strangers like the ones Ed met. To them, my deepest thanks. You build up my faith in humanity once again.

You see, miracles can still happen, and together we can end homelessness. Someday poverty will be eliminated and food banks won't be needed any longer. To you, the unknown strangers who appear on starry nights offering gifts to the poor wrapped in rags: blessings of the season to you!

52

The Gift of Christmas

THE DAY BEGINS WITH singing "Joy to the World." With the help of volunteers, we go to the street in full song for our street family. We also have the manger scene with our street family acting as shepherds, the wise men, Mary, Joseph, and the Baby wrapped in swaddling clothes, on the grassy area outside Our Place.

We offer all who pass a smile, and we invite them in for a hot breakfast. It's so rewarding to be serving in a place of hope and belonging. It's the time of Advent in the Christian calendar, a time when we wait in anticipation for the arrival of the Christ child.

This past week I was awaiting word from the finance department on the outcome of our budget for the following year. Naturally, I lose sleep over the budget; I pray that donors will come through with the donations to take us over the top. It is like waiting for the superman God, the omnipotent, all-powerful God, to swoop down and perform the miracles.

The prayer was answered, and the miracle was performed, but in the most unexpected way that once again turned my understanding of God upside down.

It was the eighth of December, and I was in the drop-in center. I had passed by him many times. David has a serious mental illness, and for at least five years, he has come in every day. He is homeless, without assistance, and has never received a mental assessment. He is low-key, not a problem to the police or to any of the front-line workers. He sits in the center day in and day out in the rags that make up his clothing, amidst the odor of his unbathed body. He is welcome there; David is in our family.

Section IV: Articles and Speeches

This morning he motioned me to come and sit by him. He just stared at me for what seemed to be the longest time before he spoke. "You have all been so good to me here at Our Place. I feel at home here, so last year I decided to save a little money for you." He went through his pockets unsuccessfully. Then he opened his backpack and dug to its bottom, and he came up with a dirty, worn-out envelope. As he handed it to me, he said, "I put one loonie away every month for you; I hope it will help." In the envelope were 12 loonies.

Yes, God appeared, not in the anticipated donor but in the beggar. The sick, weak, dirty beggar gave all he had in the true spirit of Christmas. We are not alone; God is with us in the faces, kindness, and love of our family. Advent is here not in the tinsel, the lights, or in our new iPods, but in the lowly, most unexpected ways. Open your eyes in a new way over this Advent season; look beyond what you see, and the Christ child will appear.

53

A Place of Belonging

THANKS TO THE GRACE of God and the generosity of many, we've created a place of belonging. A place of belonging is created by the smallest gestures of caring which say:

"I love you, and I'm happy to be with you at Our Place."

To create a sense of belonging, we don't just look to areas of our own self-interest, but rather, we look deeply into matters that interest others. We want them to be empowered and to feel that they belong somewhere.

In these times of economic uncertainty, more and more people are facing fear, unemployment, homelessness, hardship, and a lack of belonging. To create that belonging, Our Place will have to be in solidarity with the poor, the down-trodden, the weak, and the lonely.

This is not the time to secure our assets, retreat to safety, or withdraw our resources. No, it's a time for us to stand up and be counted, to be faithful to the vulnerable. We are called to serve. It's time to offer belonging and hope, time for us to swim upstream against the tides of self-interested protectionism and downsizing. Unfortunately, our family will grow in this time of economic uncertainty because so many out there will be faced with the loss of all their worldly possessions.

Each one of us, by answering the various calls to be part of the Our Place family, is helping to create and receive belonging. We're all called to make a real effort to grow in our own humanity and spirituality. In short, we're all called to serve others.

Section IV: Articles and Speeches

The rich and personal stories our family members share with you reveal the courage of those men and women who live with nothing but their inner strength and the grace of God. We have so much to learn from our family. We need to hear their voices, the wisdom that comes from their journeys, their struggles, and their need for a place of belonging. We've been successful this year because we've served them faithfully: welcoming them, and respecting their weaknesses, their vulnerabilities, their strengths, and their gifts.

54

Hopes and Dreams

OVER MY YEARS OF social ministry, I've found that the men and women who call the street their home each come with unique, individual histories. Not one person I've ever met had hopes and dreams, as a child or young adult, to end up begging for food or hanging around a drop-in center with an addiction problem or mental illness.

The history of many of our clients involves inner pain or relationship difficulties with parents, spouses, or friends. I've found that if I take the time to patiently listen and not jump to conclusions, my family members are yearning for relationships and for a feeling of belonging. At the same time, they fear relationships.

Yes, they cry out for love and belonging, but love and belonging makes them vulnerable and open to being hurt yet again. Breaking down the wall that they've created around themselves takes time, patience, persistence, and commitment. Their needs now are the same ones they had as children—needs that were never fulfilled. They have a strong need to have a home, a purpose, and a future. When you think about it, they're just like me. What would I do without a purpose? What would I do without a home? I'd feel rejected and despised. I'd have no self-respect and would feel like a dog just thrown a bone when I receive assistance.

We've got a lot to learn from the women and men that we serve: those I choose to call my family, those who live with us, eat with us, and seek belonging with us. Making their lives better is the essence of our work. It's through them that we've found employment. I don't know about you, but I can honestly say, "Everything I have, everything I've given to my personal family, and everything I eat is on the backs of the poor."

I've learned, therefore, to respect them, and to seek a deeper understanding of their suffering.

55

A Spiritual Question

OUR PLACE MOVES INTO its second year of operation as of January 1, 2009. We've been operating five days a week, eight hours a day for the past year, working under a philosophy of unconditional love in a non-judgmental way.

Loving someone does not simply mean doing things for them; it's so much more profound than that. To love someone is to show them their beauty and that they're important and wanted. It's to understand them, to hear their cries, to feel their struggles, and to understand their addictions, sicknesses, and weaknesses. But it's also to show them how strong they actually are. It's to rejoice and be present with them. It's spending time with them, being in their company, truly communicating with them. It's not only speaking, directing, and teaching them, but also listening, learning, and gaining insight from being with them. To love is to live in a heartfelt relationship with the other, both giving and receiving. Loving the other is empowering them so that they can take control of their own life rather than submerging them in our own preconceived conditions and goals. Loving is being honest and full of trust. It's like placing the very crystal of your heart in the hands of others and receiving, likewise, their crystal in yours.

As the work of Our Place has been unfolding, we are witnessing many examples of unconditional love: love given and received by our staff, volunteers, family members, and donors. Our Place is truly a sanctuary for many—a place where everyone is welcomed, without conditions.

Section IV: Articles and Speeches

The sign over our front door reads, "This Center has been provided by the grace of God and the generosity of others."

I've often been asked, as I walk down the streets of this city or after I have spoken to some gathering, "What can we do for you? How can we help your organization"? In love, honesty, and truth, I then ask for financial help so that next year we can open our facility twelve hours a day, seven days a week, and also provide our friends and clients with a nutritious breakfast every morning. To do this, we need 1.5 million dollars. Generous gifts from you, in these times of economic uncertainty, seem ridiculous to ask for and too selfish to be considered. Yet, out of love for those who suffer more than most of us can comprehend, I'm asking you to consider any kind of financial gift that's given from the bottom of your heart, in love.

No gift is too small. It'll take gifts from many, of all economic backgrounds, to make this dream possible. If you're someone who wishes to give but are unable to, I request that you offer up a prayer for Our Place so that others may benefit from your generosity of spirit, and our Center will become a reality for many more suffering people.

The question of bread for me is a material question, but the question of bread for my neighbor is a spiritual question.

56

The Pitcher

MOST OF YOU WILL have recently read the Times-Colonist article about the sudden and tragic death of Harley Ariana May Simpson. What you may not know is that Our Place conducts most of the street funerals in Victoria, averaging about two services a week. The service for Harley saw well over three hundred people in attendance. The guests included everyone from Mayor Dean Fortin to a homeless heroin addict whose name is Oliver. At the funeral he thanked everyone for coming on behalf of the homeless community.

Two weeks before that we did a service for Frank Williams. Frank was a major league baseball pitcher who ended up on the streets of Victoria and died at the age of 50. The Times-Colonist article stated: "Williams' life reads like a Hollywood fantasy. He was an orphan who grew up in foster homes in Seattle, but he made it to baseball's major leagues, pitching for the San Francisco Giants, Detroit Tigers, and Cincinnati Reds between 1984 and 1989. Over six seasons, he pitched 471.7 innings, had a 24–14 win-loss record with eight saves and an earned-run average of 3.00."

He crashed his car in 1989, and that event ended his playing days. I met him in 1991 when he and his brother were heavily into their alcohol addictions. I buried his brother in 2008 after he died in a fire.

"There but for the Grace of God, go I," is a well-known statement worth contemplating. Yes, it could be you, or me, or your family member. Let's not judge the weak but rather try to understand their vulnerabilities and sufferings. Let's learn to understand that they're just like us. Let's reach out to them.

As the street family gathers for these services at Our Place, we offer them a place of belonging. Our staff, volunteers, and clergy often find that, during these difficult times, we're privileged to take on the role of bereavement counselors, comforting those who have not only lost someone dear to them, but who are often themselves facing death.

Our donors also play a vital role. They arrive at these services offering gifts of sandwiches and pastries. Also, they'll often stay to comfort those who have gathered in worship.

Our Place is a loving family where we see successes and failures, joys and sorrows, beginnings and endings. It's truly a community, and the Board and I would like to thank you all for making this possible.

57

A Tribute to Melba Markel

MELBA WAS A TRUE friend in Dundela, Ontario. She could make me laugh until tears rolled down my face and my ribs ached. I'd beg her to stop just before she burst into another statement that would continue my hysteria.

She was born in Dundela and spent all of her life in and around that area. One day, when we were driving together to Montreal, she told me that Quebec was the farthest she'd ever been from her home. But not only did she live in that area, in many ways she gave her life to the surrounding district. She was a true advocate for the poor there, always standing up for them and serving them in any way that she could.

Melba was one of the founders of the House of Lazarus in the Dundela area, and she worked for the community there as a receptionist, counselor, food bank worker, and hospital visitor.

She taught me so much about the area, its history, and its people. When talking about the oppression the families of Dundela faced due to the community's judgment, she would always end up in tears. I remember asking her what I could do, and she said, "Help our young people graduate from high school. We're labeled and judged when we enter kindergarten, and not one of us has ever graduated from high school. Please help us build the proper housing that we so desperately need."

As we worked towards completing these projects, Melba was always pushing us to expand our challenges and goals. She was relentless in her drive to make sure we achieved them. Every home she lived in was kept immaculately clean, and the furnace in each place was always new or in the process of being replaced. One never had to guess where Melba stood on any issue or with any person because she'd always voice her opinion clearly and without hesitation. Joanne and Ricky were not only her beloved children—they became her best friends as they grew into adulthood. Melba stood by her friends through thick and thin and was willing to fight for them at the drop of a hat.

Beth, Myra, Melba, and I had a friendship that centered on Melba's vision of education and housing for the community that she loved. Her great sense of humor and her laughter will always live in our hearts. She'll always be in the foundation of the House of Lazarus: our teacher, my sister, and the person who could make us laugh like no other, before or after. I'll see her again someday, and until then, Heaven will never be the same. I can almost hear Jesus in full laughter as Melba joins the angels whose halos are tarnished and off kilter.

To all my family and friends in Dundela: do you realize that together we changed history? Your children continue to graduate, and some have gone on to university and college. I'm honored to call you all my family.

We couldn't have accomplished what we did, if we hadn't stood together. Tribute goes to Melba Markel, but in this tribute also hear the names of the Markel family, the Keeler family, the Lewis family, the O'Neil family, and the community of Dundela.

58

An Angel of a Different Sort

O Great Creator, this week I buried another poor, lonely, forgotten, and homeless person. Let us call her an angel of a different sort.

HER STREET NAME WAS Harley, and she was twenty years old—just a young woman, really a girl and in many ways a child. She was full of energy and would literally light up any room she entered. She was also addicted to cocaine, which on the street is called The Dragon. Although she struggled to overcome the addiction, many times The Dragon would not let her go because it had a hold on her heart, soul, and mind.

She was well known to the street population and loved by them all. She was one of those people who could be accepted into any group at any time. She was considered white, but her mother was First Nations. She'd been born into a family that was heavily addicted to alcohol, so she barely had a chance from the time of her birth. She was on the street by the age of twelve.

Her untimely death shocked us all. Late one night, she was in an altercation with two men that had just come out of a bar. One of those men pushed her in front of a bus during the fight, and she died instantly.

Those two men were not street people. They'd left the bar drunk and angry. Two of the drug addicts close by went after the men and caught them, holding them until the police arrived. The tragedy hit the front page of the newspapers. It captured the compassion of the entire city. One of the men was charged with murder two days later.

I conducted the funeral service at Our Place. More than three hundred people attended. Oliver, one of the men who had caught and restrained the man who pushed Harley, spoke at the service:

"Hi, I'm a heroin addict, homeless and sleeping on the street like an unwanted and feared rat. How do you think this makes us homeless people feel? Harley was also homeless. I knew her and loved her. I want to thank all of you for paying tribute to this fine woman. She was a homeless, forgotten, and lonely woman. I want to thank you all for attending and for your compassion. She was a believer in Jesus, and now she finally has a room in his mansion, prepared by him for her. Isn't it a shame that in this city of wealth, with the countless meetings around homelessness, we could not have found her a room? But alas, she's in no more pain. In death, her addictions have been crucified. As you leave this service, will you remember not to judge us so harshly? Can I ask that it just might be possible for you to love us as God loves you"?

After Oliver spoke, silence descended upon the funeral service. There was nothing more to say.

I then went up to the microphone and simply said, "Amen."

59

Not Alone

ADVENT IS CALLING US to prepare and to listen to the still, small voice of God in the chaos of it all. No, I'm not waiting for the superman God that I learned about as a child in Sunday school. I'm waiting for God to show her face in the strangest places—amongst the weakest, the most vulnerable, the addicted, the mentally ill, and the lonely.

We must keep our eyes open this Advent, not for a God who will suddenly emerge all-powerful, making us feel like we've won the lottery. No, we need to look for the God who will be there in a stranger or in that dim light of the fog ahead. We must open our eyes and our minds to the cracks and crevices where lost souls live in God's presence: it's in the most unlikely places that we must be open to God's still, small voice.

It's Advent. For the Christian Church around the world, it's a time of celebration—a time to celebrate homeless parents and their children who are wrapped in rags with nowhere to lay their heads. It's a time when we remember the poor shepherds coming to worship at the manger with nothing to offer but their love. It's also the time when we're called upon to remember all the poor people in the entire world: a time when the homeless, the sick, the forgotten, the hungry, and the lonely should be at the forefront of our Christian faith.

I've always been moved at this time of year, especially when I think of the timeless story of Jesus, Mary, and Joseph: how they were forced to leave their homeland and take that long journey to Bethlehem. Remember that they arrived homeless, tired, and hungry. They found refuge in a cave, hidden and not noticed by the rich or the powerful.

This morning, I was doing my usual walkabout between 5:30 and 6:45 a.m. I was on Fort St. where I usually find Kelsey, one of the old-timers, sleeping in his predictable doorway. He often wakes up the moment I stand in the door, but this morning he did not. Finally, after calling his name several times, I reached over and pulled his shoulder towards me. He awoke and poked his head outside the sleeping bag. I could immediately see the perspiration running down his face. He was wringing wet.

"Water, water, do you have any water"? he asked.

Luckily, there was one bottle of water in my van, which I'd spied earlier. I went to the van, retrieved it, and then returned to help him. I lifted his head from the cold cement, where he'd been sleeping all night long. I placed my hand under his head because he was too weak to lift it himself. His temperature was very high, and the sweat rolled relentlessly off his head. I put the water bottle to his lips, and he took several deep swallows before laying his head back down. My hand was now between his head and the cold cement.

Then I saw that look, the look of death: the blank, hollow stare that I've seen so often in my ministry. His face chilled me to the bone, yet it was a profoundly engaging look into the beyond. It mysteriously entwined our eyes, our hearts, and our souls. For a brief moment in time, we were one as he began his journey into the Spirit World.

"Rev, I'm going to die. I've been so lonely ever since they released me from jail two and a half years ago, onto the street. I've stayed alive thanks to the free food, the showers, and the love and acceptance that I found at Our Place. I'm fifty-seven, and this pneumonia will take me home, finally, to a place of rest and love. I believe that God's welcoming arms will await me."

As he spoke, I called 911, and the ambulance finally arrived. Caring paramedics put oxygen on him and tested his pulse. They gently loaded him into their vehicle. As the ambulance sounded its familiar siren cry, I stood alone once again on the sidewalk.

It was there that I realized I was experiencing a holy state. God had then appeared to me once again in the suffering around me, assuring me that I wasn't alone.

Advent is around us, if only we would open our blind eyes.

60

Cinderella and the Shoe

I WISH SO MUCH that you could come to know those living on the street: those who are often very sick, addicted, mentally ill, disabled, and lonely. Many of them are very dependent on us because of their situation and the services that we provide. I offer my stories in the hope that you'll discover the gifts and heartbeats of the very people you support.

Her name is Lee, and she's been homeless for two and a half years. She's only twenty but carries a major addiction to crack cocaine. Her health isn't good, and she now weighs only eighty pounds. She hangs out at Our Place every day, taking a shower, finding clothes that'll adorn her body, or just resting. Despite her problems, Lee brings laughter to the center by putting on clothing that makes her look ridiculous or by flamboyantly modeling a new attire.

One Monday morning, I was serving breakfast and decided to fill up some foam cups with milk and deliver them to the tables. There I was in the middle of the center carrying twelve containers of milk, when suddenly Lee backed into me, and I was wearing all twelve cups! I immediately went into the washroom to clean myself up because I was covered in milk from head to toe. Lee, however, was very upset. She began to cry and ran out of the center so quickly that one of her shoes came off. When I got out of the washroom, I was told that Lee was very distressed and had left in tears.

I grabbed the shoe that she'd left behind and went looking for her. I felt like the prince looking for Cinderella. I couldn't find her after walking several blocks, so I headed back to the shelter and began serving breakfast again. An hour or so passed before Lee returned, and in her hand was a gallon of milk.

"Rev," she said, "I didn't want anyone to go without milk."

That reaction of hers was not what I'd expect from a woman who had nothing. It reminds me of the Biblical woman giving away the only coin she had, as an offering to others. Lee reminds us that it was the greatest gift of all, for it was all that she had to offer.

61

Standing in the Rain

I STAND IN THE rain at the federal government Service Canada office at 595 Pandora Avenue, waiting to speak to the staff there about Our Place. I'm actually panhandling once again to keep Our Place operating. We must constantly keep telling our story and asking for financial help.

I'm cold and wet because this morning I gave my good *Chicago Bears* leather coat away to a young man who was wearing only a T-shirt. He'd been out all night in the rain, shivering as he approached me, soaking wet through to the skin. Without thought, I took off my treasured coat and told him to put it on.

"No, Rev, it's your coat. I can't do that."

But I continued to help him put it on and answered him, "It fits you better than me anyway, and I have another coat at home. It'd be an honor if you wore it."

His eyes filled with tears when we hugged. When the embrace was over, he turned his back and walked away in the rain. It made me think.

I thought about how easy it is to read the Book, or to quote it from the pulpit. But it's truly the most difficult piece of literature one has ever attempted to live out. C.S. Lewis wrote in *Essay Collection and Other Short Pieces*:

> I didn't go to religion to make me happy. I always knew a bottle of port would do that. If you want a religion to make you feel really comfortable, I certainly don't recommend Christianity.

"He that hath two coats let him impart to him that hath none, and he that hath food let him do likewise" (Luke 3:11 ASV).

I have found generosity very true in my ministry among the poor on the streets of Victoria. It always moves me to see the selfless sharing done by those who live in poverty. Homeless men and women often give away the little they have to others. As a child in Ottawa, I lived in poverty for most of my young life. During that time, I came to realize that poverty is not just being hungry, naked, and homeless. It also creates a feeling of hopelessness in its victims. It made me feel unwanted, unloved, and valueless. Please understand: *Poverty at its heart distorts the dreams, hopes, and potential of so many people in our community.*

When you support the Outreach Program at Our Place, you're not only making a stand against poverty and homelessness, you're also supporting the hub of hope and belonging that puts people first. The Outreach Program needs your help to support our unique services. Without you, we can't do it. Together we can do much more.

Please consider supporting the Outreach Program. Any size of gift is welcomed. For those who don't have the means to donate, I ask for your prayers. I believe that together prayer, hope, and belief can move mountains.

62

Theology

THERE WAS A TIME in my life when I wrestled for years with the Creator, wishing to put my faith behind me. When daybreak finally came, I began over a period of many years to see the Creator in a new way with a new hope.

The Creator became for me the trampled down weak Christ—a Creator without power. Jesus walked on this earth and knew our weaknesses through his own. This Creator has suffered and knows our suffering through his suffering. The Creator bears the burdens of the poor and holds no power to alleviate our suffering. The Creator instead walks with us in our despair. I discovered Christ in weak and trampled-down people: in the poor, the forgotten, the homeless, the addicted, and the mentally ill.

A passage from *Silence* by Shusaku Endo speaks directly to this discovery:

> As the priest is looking down on a crucifix with Christ upon it, he's told to trample on that crucifix in front of several poor peasants.
> "How my foot aches"! he says.
> And then Christ speaks directly to the priest: "Trample! Trample! I, more than anyone, know all about the pain in your foot. Keep trampling! I was born to be trampled on by men. The reason I carried the cross was to share in the pains of mankind."

Christ was human, as human as can be. Christ lived to love all others and would never abandon the ones who are suffering. Christ's love of others led him to his own death. The Creator walks with us, not ahead of us, but beside us. The Creator has no power to fill our cupboard with food but gives us the strength and courage to pick up our feet and walk. The Creator is not in some heaven far away sitting on a throne with some super computer to record our sins. The Creator is all around us, and the heartbeat of the Creator is *unconditional love for all.*

We have built walls to isolate and protect our "pure" faith: Christianity, Hinduism, Buddhism, Judaism, Islam, Taoism, Jainism, Sikhism, Zoroastrianism, and the Baha'i Faith are examples. In Christian history, the Creator tore down the walls of Jerusalem, threw over the tables in the temple, broke down the boundaries of our faith, and turned our thoughts upside down.

Today I believe in the Creator as a warm-hearted mother rather than as a stern-hearted, judgmental father. The Creator lives in every leaf and rock and is one with Mother Earth. The Creator finds a home in the hearts and lives of the poor, sick, and lonely.

SECTION V

Holy Rage

63

Sky's Story

Mother of God, Holy Mary, my mother prayed to you only, because she didn't feel worthy enough to pray directly to God. So, I pray to you out of desperation in the hope that you'll hear my prayer. I pray that Sky T. will find hope and a reason for living. I also pray that she'll be loved by the Creator and given enough health to see the colors of rainbows, sunsets, and sunrises.

I ARRIVED AT THE needle exchange on Cormorant Street at 6:15 a.m. I was told that Sky overdosed on heroin and consequently had no pulse. Amanda, a red-headed, female addict new to Victoria but not new to the streets, performed CPR on Sky, giving her mouth-to-mouth resuscitation and intermittently pounding on her chest to finally bring her pulse back.

An ambulance was called, and Sky was rushed to the hospital. As soon as I was told what had happened, I went to see her. When I arrived, the paramedics said that Sky would've died if it weren't for the intervention. Amanda knew well that by doing mouth-to-mouth resuscitation, she was also putting her own life in danger.

How many of us would do that, I ask, Holy Mother?

In the hospital bed, she looked so small in a fetal position, covered only by a thin, bland blue sheet. Her emaciated face was covered with sores

Section V: Holy Rage

and her skinny arm hung outside the bed, making her look like a skeleton draped with skin. When I woke her up, a slight smile came over her face.

Her doctor came to the bed when he saw me, and he said, "She's ready to go home with you now."

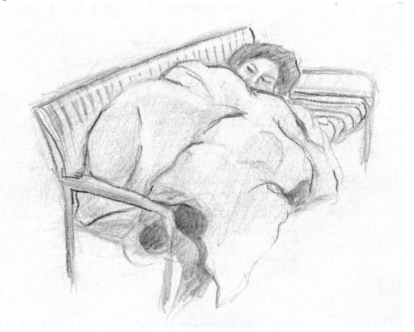

I slowly looked into his eyes and paused before telling him, "Sky is homeless. The street is her only option, so she should stay here for as long as she can. When she has to go, call me, and I'll come and get her."

The young doctor asked: "Where will you take her?"

"To her corner on a concrete sidewalk, her only home," I replied.

There was silence in the air as I turned to walk down the hall, my footsteps breaking the quietness that seconds earlier pierced our hearts. The good doctor kept her there for three more nights.

When I came to get her, one of the nurses said, "This is not a hotel, you know."

I stopped to look at her and replied, "Is it a health facility, or not"?

She didn't respond. The snide look on her face said it all.

> Holy Mother, turn our silence into a holy rage until justice flows like a mighty river and until Sky and Amanda and all their homeless friends are housed with dignity, safety, and support. Amen.

64

The Old Man

The old man is never noticed.
Passers-by just don't see him.
Perhaps it's just too painful for them,
Or maybe they're running late.

He sleeps on the sidewalk.
His worn-out, dirty sleeping bag
Reflects the life he leads.
What's at the core of his life?

We walk around or step over him,
Whatever suits us best.
Our eyes refuse to really see him,
Our hearts are cold as ice.

Some say he's mentally ill,
Others say he's addicted.
But no one stops to talk to him,
So how will we ever know the truth?

We're quick to judge him
Of course, he's at fault.
Why should we assist him?
Or look him in the eye?

Section V: Holy Rage

We're not our brother's keeper,
Why should we foot his bills?
After all, we have our own rent to pay
And food to put on our table.
We work hard to pay our bills.
Why should we care about the old man?
He's made his choices and
Reaped what he has sowed.

The Old Man

Will he remind you we're entwined
As one humanity? No one's better than the rest.
Together we must stand, or die.
Our need for one another
Is more than most will ever understand.
Until we face our own disasters,
We'll refuse to look at the old man.

After a deadly sickness in China, the whole world halts.
Hereditary Chiefs hold feathers in their hands and
Sit down on railways across our country.
Do you see the feathers in their hands?

So, the old man continues to sleep, ignored
On the hard, cold sidewalk
In his worn-out dirty sleeping bag.
The street's dirt has settled into the lines of his face.
Don't you realize it?
He's the golden thread in the tapestry of our own
humanity.

We need to open our eyes and see him.
He's part of our humanness.
The more we do for the least among us
The stronger we'll all be.
The more we stop and talk to him,
The more we'll understand his truth.
He's one of us, just another man.
Bend down, say "hello", and hear what he can teach you.
He's the golden thread of our humanity.

65

Sitting on the Fence

I'm crying out in a holy rage.

> Oh my God, I've worshipped and believed in you all my life; it was through my mother's faith that I came to know you. Yet, I now witness the suffering, judgment, and untimely death of many young adults due to drug overdoses. My questions are:
> 1. Are you still alive?
> 2. Do you hear my voice?
> 3. Do you have ears to listen to my cries?
> 4. Will my laments awaken your angels so that they can hear the cries of the poor and the oppressed?
> 5. Will you remain silent?

Janine was out there again today in a state of drug euphoria. The street calls her condition "the chicken": arms and legs uncontrollably swinging about this way and that. There she was, on her back in the grass, wailing on that small section of Pandora Avenue that separates the service road from four lanes of traffic that pour into and out of the city every day. Her legs, arms, and cries for help were uncontrollable: there she lay nearly naked for the world to see, giving us a reason to judge her.

Professionals like me are really no better than her father, who sells her body on the streets. We all watch her; we all have a history with her. We sit on the fence watching her, and we do nothing. Oh, we talk about her to one another. We talk about the homeless. We create organizations like the Greater Victoria Coalition to End Homelessness. We create other structures, and we talk about the obstacles that are in our way. We talk about finances and the commitment of governments and citizens.

We all earn our living off her situation, telling the world that we're going to solve her hell, that we're going to deal with her issues, or that we're going to find her housing. So, we set up yet another non-profit society, one after the other, all claiming to have the solution, all claiming to save her soul, or her life. The city hires more police. We give the homeless fines for sitting on the grass, resting their weary bodies. We put up more street lights. We move the homeless along from one corner to the next, but there's nowhere for them to eat on Saturdays and Sundays. All this is supported by staff, paid good salaries. Our very lives are nurtured by her suffering, her habit, her homelessness, and her addiction.

We are paid vultures in the poverty industry. What is the difference between her father and us? Our work is socially acceptable, but our salaries are sustained from the hellish life she faces. She lives for the next hit of cocaine. Her body, her mind, and her soul are given over to the dragon of death—cocaine—her drug of choice. Her father, like us professionals, also watches over her, protects her, and listens to her so that he can get some financial gain.

As I watch her from my office window, my faith is turned upside down. She's God's voice! God is alive. She's God in one of the Creator's confusing disguises, but what's difficult to say and hear is:

Section V: Holy Rage

"We remain silent."

Oh Lord, I also cry out for the church and all the outreach workers who remain silent in the face of this young woman's suffering and the suffering of so many others. I lament over my own weakness in not crying out in holy rage, but rather remaining silent, up against the system into which I have been inducted. I lament my own lack of courage to stand up and be counted: my weakness, my pride, my place of privilege in this community, which I protect. And in that protection, I, like the father, sell the girl. Oh my God, I've heard your holy rage and seen your divine presence in her battered and twisted body. I've heard your voice, and you've answered my prayers. Now I need your strength to stand up in a holy rage.

66

Alley of Death

Most days, I walk into an alley off Johnson Street. Some of the homeless, addicted, and mentally ill men and women I know had claimed it to be their bedroom. I'll attempt to bring this alley alive in this story.

I usually arrive at 6:15 a.m. I'm here to bring coffee, cookies, blankets, comfort, and companionship to those who've spent the night outside. My main reason for walking down that alley is to ensure that my street family is well. I've taken many from this place to the Jubilee Hospital's Emergency Department, often saving their lives by doing so. It's sometimes a dangerous area to visit, especially if you're new to the street.

Over the years, I've earned the respect of the homeless people who live in that alley. That's because I've been with them for a long time, and they trust me. They call me "Father" in the Catholic tradition. The walkway is narrow, and its walls are made of red brick. Many names are etched into those bricks, reminding us of the lives senselessly lost over the alley's tragic history.

After walking just ten steps into the bowels of that alley, the stink of death engulfs my nostrils like a lamb breathing in the putrid fire of a dragon. Once I've taken twenty-five steps, I'll find people lying in garbage from the dumpsters, with rats running freely over their sleeping bodies. One day as I bend over to help an old First Nations man get to his feet, the odor is just too much to take, so I hold my breath. Once he's standing and leaning on me, he begins to sing in a deep, lonely voice,

Section V: Holy Rage

"There's a house in Victoria-town they call the alley of hell. It's been the death of many a poor boy and Lord, I'll someday be one. It's the House of the Rising Sun."

His soul cries out in every word sung while two women and six men join him in the singing. But silence is my only response. That very morning, seven people lay amidst the vomit, feces, and rotting garbage. The brick walls looked like gravestones waiting for the last breaths of many. They stood silently, witnessing the acute sting of death. The air of the alley is pregnant with suffering.

Lots of people know about the alley of death. The police know, the priests know, the businessmen know, the journalists know, and the sin of their collective silence stinks to high heaven. Actually, we all know. and we watch and we cry. But, in the end, we're guilty of silence and non-action. We're implicated in the death of many.

Today, the alley has an iron gate blocking it from homeless folks. We didn't solve the problem or even seek repentance—we just moved the alley to another place.

The blood is on my hands as I sit with another person in an emergency, as she dies.

67

An Emergency

I'M NOW SITTING IN the Emergency Department of the Royal Jubilee Hospital with Jason, who's just twenty-seven years old. He's being called by the Great Spirit to join his father in the Spirit World.

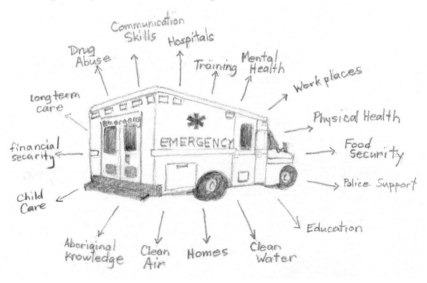

We could look at his faults and vulnerabilities and blame them on his parents or his addictions. But the question I ask as I hold his hand during the last moments of his life is,

"Are we willing to take responsibility for the failure of a social system that brought this tragedy about"?

An Emergency

I believe we cannot be silent any longer. A multitude of First Nations men and women still die at the hands of our system every day.

Our next federal election will take place on October 21, 2019. It won't be won or lost based on the character of our politicians. No—mudslinging, slander, and rumors will determine our next leaders, not the real issues at hand. And in the process, the heart and soul of who we are as Canadians will be lost. Our blindness will continue, and the mistakes of history will go unchecked. Democracy will depend on which party has the most money to convince us that the other parties are not worthy of our vote. The real issues of poverty, racial prejudice, climate change, and our inability to love one another will be lost in the rhetoric of hate. Meanwhile, marijuana and oil will lead us into the future as we continue to crucify Christ all over again.

I cannot forget the suffering in Jason's eyes. We must change the system and transform our society soon. It's an emergency.

68

Move On

Creator, I continue to search in the void for truth, for meaning, for your very existence. I continue to seek out the courage, wisdom, and love that I need to have to be with the poorest of the poor. I also seek a way to empower the poor, to liberate them, and to insist that they be given justice and a place in our community. I cry out, I lament, and I lose faith as I watch the continuing death, demoralization, and lack of love faced by the poor.

THE FOLLOWING STORY TAKES place at 5:45 a.m. and brings the above prayer into context. It comes with the language of the street. It's a profound, profane, painful, dramatic, animated language—one that captures the life, struggles, and death of the street people themselves.

As usual, I was waking up the homeless citizens of Victoria, who were sleeping in doorways, parks, and alleys.

Jay is a regular; I greet him every morning. He's been on the street a long time, and he usually sleeps in a ditch covered by a dark green tarp. He's hardly noticeable unless you're looking closely, or you've got the eyes and the heart for poor folks like I do. To do so means you have to have eyes that are sensitive to the cracks and crevices, the holes and ditches where my family put their heads to rest for the night. They are places where drunks from the bars won't urinate on them, kick them, or spit on them. As I approached Jay, he was in his usual spot, but leaning on a lamp post awaiting my arrival.

"God bless you, Reverend Al," were the first words out of his mouth. Without taking a breath, after blessing me, he continued, "Fuck, I've been evicted from houses, apartment buildings, and rat and cockroach-infested rooming houses. I've even been evicted from Street Link, the Salvation Army, and various other emergency shelters. But last night, believe it or not, I was evicted from my fucking ditch. Fuck, I am as low as a snake's belly! What is this"?

Some time passed before he spoke again. "Thanks for the warm coffee, the hug, and the smile, Reverend Al. You're always there for us, and this morning I need another hug."

Section V: Holy Rage

He continued to tell me his story. He'd lain in his ditch, putting the familiar dark green tarp over and under himself before falling asleep. Eventually he was awakened by a police officer who was grabbing the bottom of his sleeping bag and pulling him a few feet, yelling at him the whole time.

"Move on! Move on"!

He'll find another ditch or alley to sleep in tonight, but it'll only be a matter of time before he is evicted again, stated the cop. "Move on! Move on"!

I've visited fifty-eight men and women this morning: all homeless, lonely, unloved, and forgotten. Some carry a mental illness or addiction; many of them are dying. I'm like a bridge between two worlds.

Later that day, I attended a meeting of the Greater Victoria Coalition to End Homelessness. We, the community leaders, continued to talk endlessly about all the obstacles in our way, the structure that yet must be created, the partners we must secure, and the money it'll cost. Our research often falls on deaf ears, and then we begin to lose our holy rage and start to make excuses for the powers of injustice that exist in our society today. What's the bottom line?

Greed makes us want to protect our own wealth and comfort—it's that simple.

> Creator, give us the courage to seek truth and justice, the strength to love our neighbor, the power to have *holy rage*, and push us to end homelessness, hunger, and hardship. Remind us that the more we help the most vulnerable among us, the stronger our city and country will be. Oh, Holy One, light a fire under our asses.

69

Are You Useless Too?

I CALL OUT AGAIN in holy rage.

> My God, I've worshipped you all my life. Are you still alive? Do you hear my cries? Will my laments awaken your angels and summon you to hear the cries of the poor and the oppressed? Or will you remain silent, like the watchmaker who created a precious timepiece and then left his craft to the whirls and whims of the world?

I wake up the homeless people sleeping on the streets of Victoria every morning.

It was 6:00 a.m. I'd already seen twenty-five men and women in Centennial Square, adjacent to City Hall, and then on Fort Street. I pulled up to the Ministry of Housing and Social Development building on the corner of Pandora and Quadra, where another twenty-two men and women had spent the night outside. They were all addicted to various drugs. Cocaine was then the drug of choice, followed by heroin, jib (crystal meth), and rock cocaine.

I was giving out coffee and donuts, as usual. Then, out of the corner of my eye, I noticed Shane. Our history went back seven years. He had a serious personality disorder as diagnosed by his psychiatrist and had been assigned a mental health worker. However, he didn't keep his appointments so was deemed non-compliant and dropped from the worker's caseload.

Shane lived on the street in those years. Combined with his mental health issues, he was addicted to every single street drug. When I saw him that morning, he was in a doorway, crawling on his hands and knees, his

Section V: Holy Rage

face close to the ground looking intensely for whatever his mind had him looking for. I approached him slowly, saying his name well before I was close to him.

"Shane, it's Reverend Al, your friend," I kept repeating.

Finally, he noticed me and stood up, looking frightened. "Did I do something wrong"? he asked.

"No," I answered. "I just brought you a donut and a coffee."

Hesitatingly, he muttered, "Oh, thank you," before sitting down on the curb, his feet in the gutter as he stuffed the donut into his mouth like only a starving man could. I left him there alone and went about waking up others on the street that morning.

Finally, it was a quarter to seven, and I returned to the parking lot. I hopped into my car and drove it to my usual parking spot four blocks away. While walking away from my car, I went down Quadra Street and noticed Shane again. He was still crawling on his hands and knees on the sidewalk looking intensely for whatever his mind had him looking for.

He was sick and dirty, as usual. There were holes in his jeans, and his hands were bleeding. His mind was lost, yet to him I was also totally useless. The whole mental health system was useless to him.

I was so damned desperate that I cried out to God.

Are you useless too, O Lord?

It's human to blame others for the lack of care Shane is receiving. The harder question is to ask ourselves what our responsibility is to Shane.

70

I Walk Alone

I heard him crying before I saw him, behind the dumpster in a filthy alley. When he saw me, he dried his tears with the arm of his shirt, and I found myself also in tears. He used my sleeve to dry *my* eyes.

"Sit with me, Father. Let me share my tears with you."

His story unfolded as we sat together in sorrow.

"I walk alone along the dark streets of Victoria. In that darkness, I'm so alone. Ghosts from the past haunt me in my loneliness. In this deadly silence, I can hear wind rustling through the trees. I can see city rats scurrying around the gutters, overrunning the roads. But it's not the rats or the loneliness that bring fear into my heart. The piercing loneliness of the night awakens old wounds hidden inside my body, making them bleed again.

"It's the same burning fear I had when I was a child. In those days, I'd wake up in the middle of the night and run into my parents' room for comfort. But they were seldom there. Sometimes they'd leave me alone for a few hours, sometimes for days.

"I'm an adult now and no longer fear the bogeyman or the darkness of the night. It's the agonizing loneliness and bleakness that brings out the fear and tears away at my soul. The minutes of loneliness pass like hours. When I pray, I tremble in fear, and my heartfelt prayers are never answered.

"This is the lonely abyss I walk in night after night. I continually ask myself: will Mom and Dad ever return"?

He then prayed:

Section V: Holy Rage

Lord, may the sun show its face and break the spell of the wicked witch who's opened my old wounds and made them bleed like flowing water.

It was his tears that broke down my privilege and awakened me to the ghost of the past, as I walked in his shoes for the first time. That night, as I sat with him behind the dumpster, I was in the presence of the ghost of yesterday that has found a host in our souls and in those of many of my street family.

Our histories affect so many aspects of our futures.

71

Oliver

THE PURPLE-RED AND ORANGE sunrise had not yet broken through the cold winter night, but the overwhelming beauty stopped me in my tracks. There'd been bitter rain all that night, and the homeless I met were soaking wet, but not one of them was complaining. On the contrary, most of them were greeting me with smiles and grateful nods. They all needed dry socks, warm blankets, and hot cups of coffee. But what they needed most of all was a friend—someone who could look into their eyes and love them just as they are. The hope in my voice, along with my big smile and welcoming gestures, eased their loneliness for a moment. There's actually little difference between my own family and theirs. In both cases, we hunger for companionship and love; without that, the longing eats away at the very core of our being.

I saw Oliver sitting between Jazzman and Ernie on the steps of Streetlink Emergency Shelter. He was talking to both of them. He lives with them on the street and is well-loved by all the homeless people in town. I often find him listening intently to the most vulnerable and weak. Sometimes, he reminds me of a great Tibetan guru, sitting on top of a mountain, open to all who approach. The only difference is that his peak is the top of a dumpster or a bench on the streets of Victoria.

He's of First Nations descent, with a strikingly handsome face that speaks of both the depth of his spirit and the breadth of his street life. His deep, dark, large eyes hold the wisdom of Mother Earth and the compassion of his ancestors now living in the Spirit World. Some First Nations

Section V: Holy Rage

people are intrinsically white in their thinking and feel that they're one with the white world in which they've lived. It's all they've been taught, and all they know. Oliver, however, is an Indian warrior in his heart and soul. His willingness to listen to the way of his ancestors makes him compassionate to the lonely, forgotten, sick, and mentally ill. His comforting words and constant encouragement earn him the respect that a spiritual teacher would get on the street.

But Oliver isn't a saint. He lives on the street, carries a long-time addiction, and does what he has to do to survive. I call him a different kind of spirit. He lives outside the walls of society and the confines of the church, but he gives uplifting energy to all those around him. Like the disciples of Jesus, he's an outcast chased by the police. But, he's also homeless, dressed in second-hand clothing from Our Place as he sleeps on the cement steps.

If he'd been given some real opportunities and not been taken away from his parents as a child, he could have had a meaningful career. If only someone had believed in him and supported him, he could have been a social worker, a sociologist, a medicine man, or a chief. Anything would've been possible and within his grasp.

I'm proud to call Oliver a friend. For me he's a guru, a mentor, a spiritual leader, and a teacher.

What will tomorrow hold for him? Unfortunately, his history, the weight of the church, the Canadian governments of the day, and the unjust court system determined his future. The street became Oliver's home and addiction his only escape.

The Creator gave Oliver the strength of a bear, the wisdom of a wolf, and the insight of an eagle. Please challenge us to feel a holy rage against all that has oppressed Oliver and so many other homeless people.

P.S.: Oliver passed away sitting on top of an outcropping in Beacon Hill Park. His back was leaning against an old-growth tree. It was said that when he was found, two eagles were sitting atop that tree. Apparently, they stayed there for two weeks following his burial, to guide Oliver through his new journey into the Spirit World.

72

We Can No Longer Be Silent

IT'S A PARTICULAR PET peeve of mine when people start whining about how difficult or complex the homelessness problem is, saying that there are no easy solutions. That's all nonsense. All the solutions to homelessness are very simple. We need a collective will to fix the problem and a commitment to make it happen, no matter how inconvenient. The difficulty is breaking down the silos we've created—the health authority, police, social services, the legal system, corrections, and others.

I've buried far too many of our sons and daughters in Victoria over the past thirty years of my ministry. They were my extended family: the sick, the hungry, and the addicted. Many of them were homeless.

We need to come together as a society to free them and to provide wrap-around services to deal with all our issues. We need to house them properly with support. We need to create effective services for the mentally ill, the addicted, and the homeless, and we need to do it *now*. It has to become our number one priority. The more we ignore it, the more like cancer it eats away at the fabric of our society.

Every human being in this world needs a space to be inside, a place to keep their belongings and to have meaningful belongings to keep. Every human being needs to have some dignity.

How would most of us handle not having anywhere to do our business in private, to shower, or bathe? We all need to have a place to keep the world out or to have people visit.

The solution is to simply gather our collective courage and create the will to improve the lives of those more vulnerable among us. The better we are to the weakest among us, the stronger our country will be.

No more idle excuses.

I believe that freedom from poverty is a human right.

I believe in equality among all people.

I believe we're all entitled to social and economic security.

I believe in dignity for all.

Now is the time to end poverty.

It's simple:
treat the poor as if they were your mother, father,
or child.

Bibliography

Amorth, Gabriele, S.S.P. *An Exorcist Tells His Story*. San Francisco: Ignatius Press, 1999.
———. *My Battle Against Satan*. Bedford, N.H.: Sophia Institute Press, 2018.
Beckett, Samuel. *Waiting for Godot: A Tragicomedy in Two Acts*. New York: Grove, 1954.
Edison, Thomas. *Many of Life's Failures*, quoted from https://www.thomasedison.org/edison-quotes.
Endo, Shusaku. *Deep River*. Translated by Van C. Gessel. New York: New Directions, 1994.
———. *Silence*. Translated by William Johnston. London: Peter Owen, 1969.
Frost, Robert. "The Road Not Taken." In *Mountain Interval*, New York: Henry Holt, 1916.
Lewis, C.S. *Essay Collection and Other Short Pieces*. HarperCollins: London, 2000.
Peck, M. Scott, M.D. *Glimpses of the Devil: A Psychiatrist's Personal Accounts of Possession, Exorcism, and Redemption*. New York: Free Press, 2009.
Tillich, Paul. *The Courage to Be*. Fontana: Glasgow, 1952.
Tutu, Desmond. Quoted in Brown, Robert McAfee. *Unexpected News: Reading the Bible with Third World Eyes*. Westminster: John Knox 1984, p. 19.
United Church of Canada Worship Community. *Brinston and Hulbert United Church Liturgy for Holy Communion*. Toronto: United Church General Council, 1983.
Wilkinson, Tracy. *The Vatican's Exorcists: Driving Out the Devil in the 21st Century*. New York: Grand Central Publishing, 2007.

Printed in the USA
CPSIA information can be obtained
at www.ICGtesting.com
LVHW020511030724
784567LV00001B/83